THE CHALLENGE OF OUR PAST

THE CHALLENGE OF OUR PAST

Studies in Orthodox Canon Law and Church History

JOHN H ERICKSON

ST. VLADIMIR'S SEMINARY PRESS
CRESTWOOD, NY 10707–1699
1991

Library of Congress Cataloging-in-Publication Data

Erickson, John H
  The challenge of our past: studies in Orthodox Canon law and Church
history/John Erickson.
      p.   cm.
  Includes bibliographical references and index.
  ISBN 0–88141–086–1
  1. Canon law, Orthodox Eastern. 2. Orthodox Eastern Church—
Doctrines—History. 3. Sacraments—Orthodox Eastern Church.
4. Orthodox Eastern Church—Relations. I. Title.
LAW
262.9'819—dc20   · 91–11310
                                                                  CIP

©1991

ST VLADIMIR'S SEMINARY PRESS
ALL RIGHTS RESERVED

ISBN 0–88141–086–1

Typeset at St Vladimir's Seminary on a Northgate 386/20 PC
using Xerox Ventura Publisher 3.0 and a QMS PS810 laser printer
in 12pt Adobe Garamond™ on 13.5pt leading.

PRINTED IN THE UNITED STATES OF AMERICA

Table of Contents

Foreword

When I was a college student, I heard an Orthodox monk speak on the subject of "The Church in Orthodox Theological Perspective." His lecture was inspiring but also rather perplexing: roughly half of it was devoted to the Garden of Eden and the other half to the New Jerusalem of Revelation. His approach to ecclesiology, I have since discovered, is not so unusual among the Orthodox. The wealth of biblical allusions, the sensitivity to liturgy, the emphasis on the Church as mystery, the appreciation of wider theological concerns—all this has characterized much of Orthodox discussion of ecclesiology, both past and present: the many excellent modern Orthodox studies of the christological, pneumatological, trinitarian... dimensions of the Church are very much part of a tradition going back to Nicholas Cabasilas, Maximus the Confessor and beyond. But I was perplexed, and I remain perplexed; for the Orthodox Christian must be concerned about the Church not only as she truly *is* in Genesis and Revelation, at the beginning and at the end of history, but also as she meets us incarnate in the time and space of this world. Even as he looks forward to the time when the Church "will appear in its eternal glory as the Kingdom of God,"[1] the Orthodox Christian must avoid the temptation to consider the Church only in static, atemporal and otherworldly terms and take seriously the challenges posed by historical change.

The essays gathered in this volume were originally presented in widely differing circumstances to widely varied audiences. As the initial bibliographical notes indicate, most have appeared over the years as articles in scholarly journals, the earliest nearly twenty years ago. A few have been expanded or revised to take into consideration significant studies which have appeared since their original appearance, but no systematic effort has been made to bring them completely up to date.

These essays are united less by a common subject than by my own continuing interest in ecclesiological issues as these have emerged in the history of the Orthodox Church and, in particular, in its canonical tradition. They seek to investigate the ways in which certain concepts and issues relating to the Church's life have developed in the past and continue to challenge us in the present. In a sense, these could be called essays in definition. Many of them take as their point of departure certain words whose meaning and resonance has quietly but significantly shifted over the centuries—words like "canon" and "canon law" (chapter 1), "autocephalous" (chapter 7), "priesthood" (chapter 4) or "economy" (chapter 8). Others explore changes in words and images, such as those used to express the mystery of forgiveness and reconciliation (chapter 2) or to describe the Church's structures for unity and community (chapter 5, chapter 6). Still others—reflecting my continuing interest in ecumenical relations—examine changes in the issues dividing Christians of East and West (especially chapters 9 and 10); for while these essays are chiefly concerned with the ways in which the Church's unity and continuity have been perceived and expressed over the centuries, of necessity they also take into consideration problems of disunity and discontinuity.

Notwithstanding their obvious limitations, these essays do attempt to be faithful both to the eternal reality of the Church and to its historical existence. Underlying all of them is the conviction that the Church is foremost the locus for the communion of men and women with the Father through the Son in the Holy Spirit. The Church is formed and nourished by our participation in true life, in the life of the kingdom, with its radically new sense of "time" and "space"—by our participation in the very life of God—and as such it cannot be reduced to categories of the historian or the social scientist. Yet for this very reason the Church does have a social dimension. In it the *perichoresis* or "mutual indwelling" which characterizes the life of the Holy Trinity is expressed in creaturely forms. Human community is renewed. And it is within this community—in the flesh and blood, time and space of this world—that we experience the communion of the kingdom.

Also underlying these essays is the conviction that the Church cannot be adequately understood without reference to tradition. Yet discerning this tradition and its significance for the Church today is not easy.

Tradition, after all, is not just another word for church history. It is not a neat collection of texts and precedents from the past which when consulted will reveal "the Orthodox concept" or "the Orthodox doctrine" of the subject at hand. While these essays are, from beginning to end, historical, they by no means seek to glorify the past or to suggest that a history lesson will give immediately applicable solutions to all our problems. A tradition which is alive—and therefore capable even now of giving life—does not automatically assign an eternally normative or prescriptive value to what may be merely indicative or descriptive. Tradition does not make us prisoners of our own past. Rather, it reveals the Spirit at work in both past and present, so that we too, in our own time and place, may be "fellow citizens with the saints and members of the household of God, built upon the foundation of the apostles and prophets, Christ Jesus himself being the cornerstone" (Eph 2:19).

NOTES

1   V. Lossky, *The Mystical Theology of the Eastern Church* (St Vladimir's Seminary Press, Crestwood NY, 1976) 178.

Chapter 1

The Orthodox Canonical Tradition*

Few words occur more frequently in inter-Orthodox debate on ecclesiology than "canonical"—except perhaps "uncanonical." All parties constantly refer to "canons" and to "canon law," though seldom with any sensitivity to or awareness of the nature and history of the Orthodox canonical tradition itself. As a result, misconceptions abound. On the one hand, many people profess a great veneration for the sacred canons, as though the *Pedalion* fell from heaven on Pentecost, along with the *Typikon* and other such vital compendia of rules and regulations; and they look to the canons for guidance in every detail of church life. On the other hand, there are some who have an absolute aversion to canon law. For them, canon law is something to be gotten around, an arbitrary system of rules and regulations at best irrelevant to the pastoral task and even to Christianity itself, but more often positively detrimental.

The approaches of the legalist and the anarchist—if they may be so labeled—at first glance appear to be mutually exclusive. But in fact they share certain features. They have the same understanding, or rather misunderstanding, of what the canons of the Church are, and this misunderstanding in turn is based upon a misunderstanding of the nature and task of the Church itself.

Certainly the legalist is subtly but surely reducing the Church to a mere institution. He sees it as a kind of club—like the Benevolent and Protective Order of Elks or the League of Women Voters—or as the spiritual equivalent of a political unit—like the United States of America

* Originally presented as a lecture to the annual Priests' Seminar of the Orthodox Church of Finland, Kuopio, September 1982, and printed in *St. Vladimir's Theological Quarterly* 27 (1983) 155-67.

or the City of Yonkers. He sees the canons in turn as the constitution, by-laws and other regulations proper to this institution. They define the power structure and the competence of the various offices; they indicate the rights and duties of members. Thus, a person is seen as acquiring "membership" in the Church through the sacraments of baptism and chrismation, provided these are validly administered; and as long as he remains "in good standing" he is entitled to certain benefits: he may be married in the Church; he may have his home blessed with holy water at Epiphany and his basket of sausages and fancy breads blessed at Easter; he may receive a Christian burial and prayers for the repose of his soul upon departing this life. All this and more: he becomes eligible, as it were, for membership in the kingdom of heaven. But there are certain requirements that must be met. Not too many years ago, the faithful would typically be reminded each Lent of the importance of fulfilling their "annual obligation" of confession and communion. And there are certain rather arbitrary rules governing behavior and procedures that must be followed. Thus, a member of the Orthodox Church may marry once, twice and, in certain circumstances, thrice; but never four times.

This sketch of the legalist's understanding of the Church is, to be sure, exaggerated. Virtually everyone would admit in principle that the Church is not just another club or political entity. It is, after all, distinguished by its exalted Founder. Few know or care who founded this or that fraternal organization. While we do speak of the "founding fathers" of our country, we do not accord them the honors due the Founder of the Church, Jesus Christ. Further, the Church is distinguished by its exalted purpose. It offers man forgiveness of sins, salvation, eternal life—not just good fellowship or the chance to promote a worthy cause or the myriad benefits of the welfare state. Yet even if the Church's exalted Founder and purpose are duly acknowledged, there is still something lacking in this approach. The Church is still seen above all as an institution, as a society that operates in much the same way as other societies, even though it may be incomparably superior to them. It is seen in terms of its organization, its structure, while its purpose is ignored or misconstrued. After all, man is called to communion with God, not just to have a valid baptism, a nice church wedding and finally memorial services on the ninth day, the fortieth day and the anniversaries of his death. Man is called to participation in God, to be by participation what God is by nature, so that even the salvation offered by the Church is not just so many doses of this grace or that, duly administered through proper channels. It is not some external benefit, whether for this life or the next; much less is it a reward for following all the rules and regulations. It is above all a living personal relationship with God; it is life that is truly life because it is participation in the divine life itself, because it is a life of communion.

We must beware, therefore, of the misconceptions of legalism. But what of that other position, which for the sake of convenience we labeled anarchism? As suggested earlier, many regard canon law as utterly alien to the spirit of the New Testament and to that freedom in Christ of which St Paul often speaks. We live under the gospel, they proclaim, not under the law; under the new dispensation, not the old. This attitude, so widely encountered, does not require elaboration. And that it does not accurately reflect the thought of St Paul and of the other writers of the New Testament is, I believe, obvious. When Paul speaks of freedom, he means above all freedom from slavery to sin, death and the devil. While he does reject any reliance on the Mosaic law, particularly in its ritual elements, in almost the same breath he can tell the Galatians to "fulfill the law of Christ" (6:2).

Less obvious is the fact that the anarchist's attitude does not accurately reflect the spirit of the canons. Many of our canons are opposed—deliberately and explicitly—to the narrow legalism of the Mosaic law. For example, Leviticus 21:17-21 excluded from priestly ministry anyone having a physical deformity: "he shall not come near the veil or approach the altar, because he has a blemish, that he may not profane my sanctuaries" (21:23). Compare this to canon 77 of the so-called Apostolic Canons: "If anyone be deprived of an eye, or lame of a leg, but in other respects be worthy of a bishopric, he may be ordained, for the defect of the body does not defile a man, but the pollution of the soul."[1]

Note also the canons dealing with penitential discipline. Their provisions are quite unlike those of most penal codes, in which penalties are mechanically laid down in proportion to the gravity of the offense. Instead, the canons stress the disposition of the penitent, his entire spiritual state; and the penances prescribed are understood as essentially medicinal rather than vindicative: they are cures for the disease that is sin, not the Church's version of "doing time" or "paying a debt to society."

The anarchist, then, has misread the canons, or more likely he has not read them at all. But there is another, deeper defect in his understanding of the Church and its canons. The legalist, as I have suggested, sees the Church only as institution and either neglects its purpose or distorts it to fit his own preconceptions. The anarchist, on the other hand, is convinced that he understands and pursues the purpose, but he finds that the Church as institution, with all its canons, is irrelevant or possibly even harmful to this purpose. He believes that the real task of the Church—and of the priest—is to "help" people with all their many problems—"help" usually being defined in terms purloined from the social worker or the psychiatrist—and that the institution is something to be circumvented, a power structure with no necessary relation to the task that it is supposed to be performing. We come to a fundamental question: what ultimately is the relationship of the Church's structures to its saving task? Are the Church's structures and norms of behavior (i.e., its canons) simply arbitrary, with no intrinsic connection to the Church's task of making present to man God's saving activity? Do we have them simply because they can be convenient or useful, like laws that tell us to drive on the right side of the road rather than the left? In examining the anarchist's position, we thus end up asking much the same question that we raised earlier in connection with the legalist's position: to what extent is the Church a society like other societies, governed by a body of laws analogous to those of other societies?

Undeniably, the conception of the Church as a quasi-political society can be traced to the Bible itself. The very word for Church, *ekklêsia*, has important political connotations. In secular Greek usage the word does not simply mean the community understood as a collection of individuals, the sum total of the citizenry, but rather describes their gathering as a body politic—its etymology suggests a community being "called out" to an assembly. The translators of the Septuagint therefore used *ekklêsia* to render the Hebrew word *qahal*, which referred to the community of Israel assembled at God's call, to those whom God called out of Egypt and gathered in the desert as His chosen people.

This kind of sociopolitical imagery occurs frequently in the New Testament and in patristic literature, though nowhere is it pursued with the singlemindedness of Cardinal Bellarmine, who in the sixteenth century saw the Church as "a single, concrete historical society, having a constitution, a set of rules, a governing body, and a set of actual members who accept this constitution and these rules as binding on them ... a society as visible and palpable as the community of the Roman people, or the kingdom of France, or the Republic of Venice."[2] But does this imagery fully and adequately express what the Church truly is? Does it, as Cardinal Bellarmine apparently thought, provide sufficient material for a complete definition of the Church? The New Testament and patristic literature in fact apply a wide variety of images to the Church: it is the ark, the building on a rock, the virginal mother, the new creation, the heavenly Jerusalem ... , but above all there is the organic Pauline imagery of the Church as the body of Christ and the sacramental imagery of the Gospel according to St John. These images do not exclude the political image or deny its importance, but they do serve to supplement, correct and clarify it. The Church is indeed a society, the people of God, but precisely because the Church is sacrament, the effective sign and presence of the kingdom which is to come. The Church is not an autonomous, self-directing society established long ago to dispense grace and make and break its own rules until Christ comes again in glory. The thrust even of the New Testament's political imagery is eschatological: the Church is that chosen race, royal priesthood and holy nation foretold by the prophets for the last times (1 Pt 2:9). The accent is on fulfillment. If the Church can be described as a perfect society, this is not because of a constitution laid down long ago by its Founder but because it effectively participates in the ultimate realities that it signifies. In other words, the Church is not just a horizontal community; it is also a vertical communion. And it is this life of communion that makes possible life as community, as the people of God. From this it follows that the Church's "constitution" is qualitatively different from those of other societies. It is not an extrinsic collection of rules laid down by the appropriate legislator. Rather, the Church's structures and norms of conduct necessarily arise from and conform to its nature as the Spirit-filled body of Christ.

This point is illustrated very clearly in 1 Corinthians, where virtually every aspect of church life and personal conduct is referred to the mystery of Christ. On quarreling, Paul asks: "Is Christ divided?" (1:11); on behavior at the eucharistic gathering, he reviews the words of institution (11:17-26); on immorality: "Your bodies are members of Christ. Shall I therefore take the members of Christ and make them members of a prostitute?" (6:15); on idolatry: "You cannot drink the cup of the Lord and the cup of demons. You cannot partake of the table of the Lord and the table of demons" (10:21); on church structure: "Now you are the body of Christ and individually members of it. And God has appointed in the Church first apostles, second prophets, third teachers ... " (12:27-8). St Paul touches upon many problems that we might describe as "canonical," but his approach is not that of "canon law" as defined in modern textbooks: "the body of law constituted by legitimate ecclesiastical authority for the proper organization and government of the church as a visible society."[3] For him, the "visible society" has its rules, but they cannot be considered apart from the invisible realities to which they refer and from which they derive their meaning.

With St Paul we are far from the misconceptions of the legalist and the anarchist but close the meaning that "canon" had in the early Church. The word was not yet imbued with the notions of legal positivism; it did not mean an ecclesiastical law duly enacted and promulgated for his "jurisdiction" by the competent legislator—be that bishop, synod, pope or ecumenical council. In secular usage it originally referred to a straight rod or line, like the plumb line used by surveyors to determine true vertical. Hence, "canon" meant "rule," not in the sense of regulation or habitual practice, but rather in the sense of a straightedge, a "ruler": an absolute standard for straightness or measurement. By extension, it meant a standard for determining the correctness of an action or belief. Thus, early Christian writers often refer to the "canon" or "rule" of faith—i.e., the Creed—and we also find references to the Christian canon or rule of behavior: "Peace and mercy be upon all who walk by the canon, upon the Israel of God" (Gal 6:16). "Canon" therefore suggests an absolute and universal rule or standard as old as the Church itself and handed down as part of tradition. In his "canonical epistles" St Basil the Great constantly refers to the canons as "what we have learned from the ancients," "what we have been taught," or "what the fathers have handed down to us" (literally, "traditioned to us"). To be sure, a canon may have to be restated or reformulated from time to time in view of particular circumstances, but that does not mean that it was "made," whether by St Basil or any other "legislator." "It was a rule of the universal Church and had always been so. It had been observed everywhere since the time of the apostles, and if it had been 'made' it was made by them. After that, it was simply 'found.'"[4]

This stress on the traditional character of the canons is particularly strong in the so-called "apostolic church orders"—the *Didachê*, the *Apostolic Tradition* of Hippolytus, the *Didascalia Apostolorum* and similar works that purport to come from the apostles themselves. They are of course products of a later period and were compiled to meet particular needs. Yet their provisions are invariably expressed in terms suggesting universal application. "When therefore the whole Church was in peril of falling into heresy, all the twelve apostles came together to Jerusalem and took thought what should be done. And *it seemed good to us, being all of one accord,* to write this catholic instruction," asserts the *Didascalia Apostolorum.*[5] Also noteworthy is the way in which these works link canonical matters with the liturgy. The Church as community is not considered apart from its worship and sacramental life. Thus, even discussion of church finances—first-fruits and tithes—is accompanied by appropriate prayers (*Apostolic Tradition* 28). The *Didascalia Apostolorum* deals at length with what might be described as ecclesiastical court procedure, but in its usual hortatory style it links the topic explicitly to eucharistic fellowship: "Now the gift of God is our prayer and our Eucharist. If then thou keep any malice against thy brother, or he against thee, thy prayer is not heard and thy Eucharist is not accepted ... Wherefore, O bishop, that your oblations and your prayers may be acceptable, when you stand in the Church to pray let the deacon say with a loud voice, 'Is there any man that keepeth aught against his fellow?'"[6] Similarly, the *Apostolic Tradition* links rules for Christian conduct with discussion of the catechumenate and then proceeds directly to prayers and rubrics for baptism and the eucharist. In a striking fashion, Christian moral demands are placed within the broader context of the paschal mystery—baptism into Christ and participation in His body.

We find the traditional character of the canons also emphasized in the "decretal letters" of the popes of Alexandria (extant from the late third century onward) and of Rome (extant from the late fourth century onward). Unlike the apostolic church orders, these decretal letters do not attempt to provide a complete guide to church life and worship. They deal rather with specific problems, such as restoration of the lapsed and other sinners to eucharistic communion. They suggest the growing authority of the major sees, and some of the Roman letters make use of what are unmistakably legislative formulas. But for the most part, even when dealing with new situations, they do not attempt to "make" laws but rather to "find" the Church's canon, whether in scripture or in tradition.

The same holds true for earlier conciliar activity. Whether considering specific problems in church life or arbitrating disputes and judging cases, the councils claimed to be simply following and applying the age-old canons. If an issue was especially significant or if it affected a number of churches, it might be desirable or necessary to restate the canon and show its application to the case at hand. Thus, canon 10 of the Council of Nicea reads:

> If any who have lapsed have been ordained through the ignorance, or even with the previous knowledge of the ordainers, this shall not prejudice the canon of the Church; for when they are discovered they shall be deposed.

It might also be useful to mandate new practical measures to insure the effectiveness of the canon. A case in point is Nicea, canon 5:

> Concerning those, whether of the clergy or of the laity, who have been excommunicated in the several provinces, let the provisions of the canon be observed by the bishops which provides that persons cast out by some be not readmitted by others. Nevertheless, inquiry should be made whether they have been excommunicated through captiousness, or contentiousness, or any such like ungracious disposition in the bishop. And, that this matter may have due investigation, it is decreed that in every province synods shall be held twice a year ...

"It is decreed..." —we move almost imperceptibly toward the idea of the canon as a piece of legislation. Nicea and the other councils of the earlier fourth century still generally refer to their own measures as *horoi*, "decisions," rather than "canons," but by the time of the Council of Constantinople in 381 usage is beginning to shift (canon 2). The term "canon" is being "extended from the rule which the synods were supposed to be stating to their statement of the rule."[7]

Collections of these conciliar statements were made from the fourth century onward. Of these, the most important is that associated with the

Church of Antioch, which forms the nucleus of the present Orthodox canonical corpus. The canons of Nicea are given first place; they are followed by those of Ancyra, Neocaesarea, Gangra, Antioch and Laodicea; and later those of Constantinople and Ephesus were added. This collection enjoyed wide circulation, and its position as a veritable code of canon law for the imperial Church was confirmed by the Council of Chalcedon: "We have judged it right that the canons of the holy fathers made in every synod even until now, should remain in force" (canon 1). A canon now is understood above all as a rule made by a council.

This shift in the meaning of "canon" is but one aspect of the veritable metamorphosis that the canonical tradition underwent following the conversion of Constantine and the establishment of Christianity as the favored, and then the official, religion of the Roman Empire. The Church came to enjoy many of the rights, privileges, exemptions and benefits that the pagan cults earlier had enjoyed under public law. In turn, however, its "constitution" and structures had to be clearly defined and expressed in terms of law, if only because government officials needed to know who legally represented the Church. Here earlier canonical literature was unsatisfactory, for it seldom laid down precise requirements—"Let a bishop be ordained by two or three bishops" (Apostolic Canon 1)—tending instead to be maximalist in vision and categorical in tone. St Cyprian writes:

> You must diligently observe and keep the practice delivered from divine tradition and apostolic ordinance, which is also maintained among us, and almost throughout all the provinces, that for the proper celebration of ordinations all the neighboring bishops of the same province should assemble. (*Ep.* 67)

"*All* the neighboring bishops ... " But in the fourth century this perforce begins to change. Consider Nicea, canon 4:

> It is by all means proper that a bishop should be appointed by all the bishops in the province; but should this be difficult, either on account of urgent necessity or because of distance, three at least should meet together ...

Alongside the traditional canonical maximalism, minimum requirements are being established, sometimes by ecclesiastical authorities, as in this canon, but often by the imperial authority. Justinian's famous Novella 6, for example, whose prologue so eloquently describes the *sacerdotium* and the *imperium* as "God's two great gifts to man," in fact is a complete set of by-laws for the Great Church of Constantinople.

Ecclesiastical canons and imperial laws define church structure and procedure more precisely and in greater detail, but with less attention to their ultimate purpose. Take, for example, episcopal arbitration of disputes. Earlier canonical literature had seen this as one element in the maintenance of eucharistic fellowship within the local church. Now imperial legislation has made episcopal arbitration legally binding on all who avail themselves of it. Bishops complain that every morning is consumed in hearing litigation. Even non-Christians hasten to the bishop's court because of its reputation for settling disputes faster and more even-handedly than the civil courts. In short, the bishop's court has come to play an important role in establishing and maintaining society at large on a sound Christian basis, but eucharistic communion is no longer its focus or raison d'être.

In Byzantium the process begun with the conversion of Constantine reaches its apogee. Never before or since has the world been so completely open to the Church and its message. Conversely, never before or since has the Church been so completely open to the world. A book on the Byzantine Church might well take as its epigraph a phrase from canon 38 of the Synod in Trullo (692): "Let the order of things ecclesiastical follow the civil and public models." It would be misleading and inaccurate to speak of caesaropapism at this point, for we are not dealing with two entities, "church" and "state," one totally external to the other and therefore capable of dominating it or for that matter of entering into concordats with it. Rather, there is a full participation of the Church in the life of the empire and full participation of the empire in the life of the Church.

Nowhere is this interpenetration more evident that in the "nomocanons"—i.e., those collections in which both ecclesiastical canons and civil laws (*nomoi*) are presented according to topic. These collections had several features that made them especially useful to bureaucrats, whether ecclesiastical or civil. They made it possible to see at a glance which canons and civil laws dealt with a given subject: the hierarchy, clerical discipline, obligations of the faithful, etc. In addition, their canonical sections were as comprehensive as possible. For example, the sixth-century *Syntagma in Fourteen Titles*, on which the famous *Nomocanon in Fourteen Titles* is based, includes such diverse texts as the eighty-five so-called "apostolic canons," the "canonical epistles" of St Basil and other holy fathers and the lengthy African Code in addition to the conciliar canons of the old code of the imperial Church. In other words, it includes all those "canons" to which the Synod in Trullo would later ascribe ecumenical authority (canon 2).

Yet for all their practical advantages, the nomocanons present a serious hermeneutical problem. *Kanones* are still nominally distinguished from *nomoi*, and in case of disagreement they are to be given preference, according to canonists like Balsamon. Yet they are distinguished not so much by their form, substance or purpose as by the agency that has enacted them. Lost is the early Church's sense of canon as part of the tradition, absolute and universal, maximalist in its vision of church life. Instead, canons are understood to be laws on ecclesiastical matters duly made and promulgated in written form by the competent ecclesiastical authority as distinct from the civil authority. As such, they may be interpreted and applied analogously to the *nomoi*. They may be codified in much the way that the great Justinian codified the civil law, and they may be commented upon by legal experts accustomed to all the techniques of civil law commentary—paraphrase, scholia, aporiae, etc.

This process of fusion and confusion of *kanôn* and *nomos* continues in late Byzantium with works like the *Syntagma* of Matthew Blastares, which in a crude but effective manner arranges canons and laws side by side, alphabetically by topic. But it reaches its fulfillment in the millet system of the Turkocratia, in which the Orthodox community was administered by a single authority—the ecclesiastical, according to the canons and the old imperial laws. The situation in Russia after Peter the Great, though seemingly altogether different, in fact simply presents the reverse of the same coin: the Orthodox community is ruled by a single authority—the civil, which is sovereign over both spiritual and secular aspects of society. Whether in Istanbul or St Petersburg, the double-headed eagle remained a particularly pertinent symbol.

Absorption into the world, into culture, into national life, is a temptation to which the Orthodox Church certainly has not been immune. If it has not succumbed to it completely, after the manner of nineteenth-century *Kulturprotestantismus*, this is because a certain transcendent, indeed eschatological element has been maintained, above all by the monastic tradition. As the late Fr Georges Florovsky so neatly demonstrated, monasticism became a "permanent resistance movement" within the Christian empire, just as the Church itself had been within the pagan empire.[8] And as heir to the Church of the martyrs and confessors, monasticism also was heir to its imagery. When the Constantinian settlement gave unprecedented occasion for elaboration and application of what I have termed the "political" image of the Church, other images might well have been quietly discarded or else left to schismatics like the Donatists: the strong tower of refuge, the ark of Noah well-tarred to keep out the defiling waters of the world... Instead, they come to be applied to monasticism or, internalized, to the life of the soul. It was not forgotten that the Christian's true patria is the kingdom of heaven; that his true life depends on communion with God and not just on valid membership in the Christian community. Yet the implication of life-as-communion for life-in-community were seldom pursued, at least not beyond the cloister walls. Instead, we find hints of an elitism that would contrast or even oppose the "real" Church of spiritual experience and personal piety to the institutional Church. This is what Nicetas Stethatos, disciple of St Simeon the New Theologian, has to say:

> For he is bishop in the eyes of God and the Church of Christ, who has been revealed in the Church by the Holy Spirit as a theologian (*theologos*), rather than he who has received the episcopal ordination from men but still needs initiation (*mystagogian*) into the mysteries of the kingdom of heaven ...[9]

There are, of course, exceptions—witness the social dimensions of the late Byzantine spiritual renaissance or the powerful impact of St Sergius on Russia. Yet even these exceptions prove the rule. We know how quickly disputes between the "possessors" and the "nonpossessors" divided and then dissipated the spiritual patrimony of St Sergius.

*   *   *   *

We Orthodox Christians today desperately need to rediscover the implications of communion for community, lest our much-vaunted "spirituality" and "mystical theology" degenerate into dilettantish escapism, and our church community into that caricature idolized by the legalist and scorned by the anarchist. In this task of rediscovery, the canonist can play an important role, but only if he learns how to "read" the canons correctly. He cannot imitate the legalism of the classic Byzantine canonists, for whom it was enough to cite the text, chapter and verse, and then resolve any apparent contradictions by wooden application of certain arbitrary hermeneutical rules—the canon of an ecumenical council takes precedence over one of a local council, a later canon takes precedence over an earlier one, etc. Nor can he simply ignore the canons when it seems expedient, justifying his actions by appeals to pastoral discretion or "economy." He must read the canons in the light of history, but at the same time he must avoid the occupational hazards of the historian: relativism and cynicism. Above all, he must go beyond "canons" and "canon law" to the "canon" as that word was understood in the early Church. He must search out those norms for structure and conduct that necessarily arise from and conform to the very nature of the Church as the Spirit-filled body of Christ. Only by applying this hermeneutical principle will he be able to go beyond the misconceptions of legalist and anarchist and discover the hidden riches of the Orthodox canonical tradition.

NOTES

1 Here and throughout this essay, translations of the canons are taken from *The Seven Ecumenical Councils,* A Select Library of Nicene and Post-Nicene Fathers, 2nd ser, vol 14, unless otherwise noted.

2 Quoted by A. Dulles, in *Models of the Church* (Doubleday, Garden City, NY 1974) 39.

3 *New Catholic Encyclopedia* 3 (New York 1967) 29.

4 J. Taylor, "Canon Law in the Age of the Fathers," in *Readings, Cases, Materials in Canon Law,* ed J. F. Hite, G. J. Sesto and D. J. Ward (The Liturgical Press, Collegeville, MN 1980) 40.

5 Ed and tr R. H. Connolly (Oxford 1929) 214.

6 Ibid. 117.

7 Taylor, 46.

8 In his essay "Empire and Desert: Antinomies of Christian History," *Greek Orthodox Theological Review* 3 (1957) 133-59.

9 *On the Hierarchy* 5:37, ed J. Darrouzès, *Sources chrétiennes* 81 (Paris 1961) 340; see J. van Rossum, "Reflections on Byzantine Ecclesiology," *St Vladimir's Theological Quarterly* 25 (1981) 78.

Chapter 2

Penitential Discipline in the Orthodox Canonical Tradition*

The subject of this essay calls for little explanation or apology. Few in the Orthodox Church today would question the need for investigation of the history of penitential discipline in the Orthodox canonical tradition. Yet the task is not an easy one. No other sacramental act of the Church has undergone such extensive developments and changes in its outward forms. Most of the other rites of the Church attained their present form, or something closely resembling it, by the eleventh century, but the penitential rite was undergoing development well into the eighteenth. Even today many variations can be found, the most noteworthy being that between the indicative formula of absolution ("I absolve thee ... ") employed in the Russian Church and the deprecative formula ("May God forgive ... ") followed elsewhere. And corresponding to these many changes and variations in external form are a profusion of theoretical problems. With some trepidation, then, I should like to begin this presentation with a few generalizations concerning the practice and understanding of penance in the Church to the mid-fourth century, passing over the various penitential disputes of Christian antiquity in silence, dismissing as red herrings many of the problems and pseudo-problems posed by modern scholarship, and ignoring the considerable variation of penitential practice and institutions from place to place and time to time during this period.

Penance in the Early Church

Penance in the early Church is a comparatively well-explored subject— and also one that has provoked considerable controversy. The older view

* Presented at the annual meeting of the Orthodox Theological Society in America, May 1977, and originally printed in *St Vladimir's Theological Quarterly* 21 (1977) 191-206.

of Harnack *et al.*—that an early Christian rigorism, which allowed no possibility of reconciliation to the Church of those guilty of the capital sins of murder, fornication and apostasy, gradually gave way to laxism—has been challenged and now is largely discredited, or at least subject to considerable revision and modification.[2] The Church has always known the power of the keys and has not known limits to this power—at least not limits imposed by the relative greatness of the sin. But for the first centuries of the Church's life, few occasions for controversy arose. The early Church know few post-baptismal murderers or fornicators. Their "second baptism" by the baptism of repentance therefore is rare. What did prove a problem was apostasy. Already in the correspondence between Pliny the Younger and the Emperor Trajan we read of those who "said that they were Christians and then denied it, explaining that they had been, but ceased to be such, some three years ago, some a good many years, and a few even twenty" (Pliny, *Ep.* 10.96.6). But such people rarely returned to the Church—not that they were excluded on principle from repentance and reconciliation, but they excluded themselves: they did not repent. An acute problem arises only with the Decian persecution (250-1), which followed nearly a half century of peace for the Church. The situation is dramatically depicted by St Cyprian in his treatise *On the Lapsed* and in his letters. Families are divided: a son dies as a martyr, but his mother and sister apostasize (*Ep.* 27.1). "Born Christians" rush to sacrifice and as quickly beg—or demand—restoration to that society whose benefits they had so long enjoyed. Penitential discipline becomes a large-scale and immediate problem not only in Cyprian's Carthage but throughout the empire, and following the even harsher persecutions under Diocletian (from 302) the problem recurs.

I have reviewed church history at this point because it was precisely in this period that the canonical tradition in matters of penance was being formed. Or, to put it slightly differently, the reconciliation of apostates becomes the model for the sacrament of penance in the early Church, particularly for the period immediately preceding and immediately following the Council of Nicea.[3] It is essential, therefore, to analyze the chief characteristics of the practice and understanding of penance in this period.

(1) To many, the most noteworthy feature of penitential discipline in

antiquity is the length and severity of the penances prescribed. For example, canon 22 of the Council of Ancyra (314) prescribes: "With regard to willful homicides, let them be 'prostrators,' and deemed worthy of the eucharist only at the close of life." And depending on their own proclivities, they are appalled either at the severity of antiquity or at the laxity of modern times. Yet this is misleading. In fact, there was considerable variety on this point. Penances prescribed in the canonical epistle of St Peter of Alexandria (d. 311), for example, are in no case very extended or of an extreme character, even for the lapsed. What is more impressive, though perhaps less obvious from the bare bones of our canonical texts, is the definite ecclesial context of penance in this period. A few passages from the *Didascalia Apostolorum*, a third-century Syrian compendium of instruction and admonition for bishops, may illustrate what I mean by this:

> Judge therefore, O bishop, strictly as God Almighty; and those who repent receive with mercy as God Almighty. And rebuke and exhort and teach; for the Lord God also with an oath promised forgiveness to them that have sinned ...

> But when thou hast seen one who has sinned, be stern with him, and command that they [i.e., the faithful] put him forth; and when he is gone forth let them be stern with him, and take him to task, and keep him without the Church; and then let them come in and plead for him ... And then do thou, O bishop, command him to come in, and examine him whether he be repentant. And if he is worthy to be received into the Church, appoint him days of fasting according to his offence, two or three weeks, or five, or seven; and so dismiss him that he may depart, saying to him whatever is right for admonition and instruction; and rebuke him, and say to him that he be by himself in humiliation, and that he beg and beseech during the days of his fast that he may be found worthy of the forgiveness of sins ...[4]

> But thou shalt by no means forbid them to enter the Church and hear the word, O bishop; for neither did our Lord and Saviour utterly thrust away and reject publicans and sinners, but did even eat with them ... and afterwards, as each one of them repents and shows the fruits of repentance, receive him to prayer after the manner of a heathen. And as thou baptizest a heathen and then receivest him, so also lay hands upon this man, whilst all pray for him, and then bring him in and let him communicate with the Church ...[5]

We have here not just the reconciliation of the individual sinner with his God, but—congruent with this—his reconciliation with the Church, with the bishop standing in the place of God, acting as His steward, His *oikonomos*, and with all the faithful actively involved in intercession.

(2) The context of penance is the Church; its goal, the eucharist. This orientation can be seen in countless texts, whether canonical or liturgical, historical or dogmatic. One illustration is a canon which summarizes the system of graded penance introduced by St Gregory the Wonderworker in Pontus (*Can. ep.* canon 11):

> The grade of "mourner" takes place outside the door of the church; here it is proper for the sinner to stand, and to beseech the faithful as they enter to pray for him. That of "hearer" is inside the door, in the narthex; here it is proper for the sinner to stand as long as the catechumens remain, and then to go forth. For he [Gregory] says, when he has heard the Scriptures and the instructions, let him be put forth and not be counted worthy of the prayer. The grade of "prostrator" is when he stands within the door of the nave, and goes forth with the catechumens. That of "stander" is when he takes his stand with the faithful, and does not go forth with the catechumens. Last is that of participant in the Holy Things.

Penance here is seen as an ordered process or movement of return to eucharistic communion. The system of St Gregory, apparently confined to Pontus, Cappadocia and parts of Asia, is noteworthy for its articulation, but analogous provisions can be found virtually everywhere. Special prayers, special clothing, special gestures and postures made the penitent as much a feature of the early Church as the catechumen, to whom he is often compared, arousing—as in the case of Fabiola in Rome—the admiration and awe of the community or—as in the case of some in St Augustine's Hippo—the suspicion that they would as soon remain penitents as return to communion (cf. *Hom.* 232.8).

(3) As we note this ecclesial context and eucharistic orientation, we should also note what is absent: an inquisitorial procedure, an established pattern for "confession." To the dismay of an older generation of polemicists, whether Roman Catholic or Protestant, texts of this period show little interest in confession as such, whether "public" or "private." For the most part, our texts suppose that the sin itself was manifest, known to all. The penitential system of the early Church, patterned, as it were, on the paradigmatic sin of apostasy, presupposes what might be called *the objective nature of sin*. Sin is not just a disposition, an inclination, a psychological state. Rather, the sinner, operating in full knowledge, makes a deliberate, conscious choice, and completes this movement of the will

with an act that manifestly excludes him from the body of the faithful and identifies him with the works of the Evil One. He abandons the banquet of immortality for the libations of idols—often literally. The whole man is involved. So also, penance itself involves not just a change in attitude, but calls for the fruits of repentance, manifested in diverse outward ways. Among these—along with prostrations, sackcloth and ashes—is confession (*eksomologêsis*). It is chiefly a penitential exercise, one of the fruits of repentance, and not part of a judicial procedure. For a judicial procedure was not really considered necessary. I am reminded of the last of the synods against Paul of Samosata, that third-century heretic: "There is no need for any judgment first upon his deeds, since he is outside; he has departed from the canon ... "[6] (I add parenthetically that there was likewise no set formula for "absolution." Certainly there were prayers over the penitents, and some texts like the *Didascalia Apostolorum* speak of a final imposition of hands by the bishop. But absolution was above all signaled by a return to eucharistic fellowship. Very often one simply reads that a person is to "proceed to communion" [Laodicea canon 2] after completing the prescribed penance, that he is "then to undertake the communion of the Good" [Basil the Great canon 4].)[7]

This penitential system of the early Church has its strengths: a clear understanding of the relationship between penance and the eucharist, an awareness of the ecclesial dimension of penance and reconciliation, a strong insistence on repentance and its fruits. But it also has certain manifest weaknesses. There is the obvious danger of a wooden legalism, according to which penance is viewed as "doing your time," as "paying your debt to society"—a danger that becomes particularly acute if a eucharistic orientation of penance is lost. Further, the intimate connection between thought, will and act presupposed in the apostasy model can break down in a number of ways. Thought does not always lead to assent of the will; a movement of the will is not always completed by action; ignorance, fear, compulsion or sheer stupidity can always intervene. The various ancient canons and theological writers dealing with penance are forced to consider such problems, but they often show an extraordinary lack of sensitivity. (For example, canon 4 of the Council of Neocaesarea declares: "If any man lusting after a woman purposes to lie with her, and his design does not come to effect, it is evident that he has been saved by

grace.") And what of secret sins, spontaneously confessed to the priest or
bishop and not known to all? Public penance can also involve, in the
words of St John Chrysostom, "the intolerable publicity of the forum"
(*Hom. contra Anomeos* 5). It can involve legal difficulties. Canon 132 of
the African Code reports a painful case: a man confesses to his bishop in
secret, is publicly penanced, but then recants and accuses the bishop of
defamation of character. It can even involve physical danger. For this
reason Basil the Great (canon 34) makes special provisions for the secret
adulteress:

> Our fathers did not command public exposure of women who have committed
> adultery and have confessed through godly fear [i.e., secretly] or were convicted
> in some other way, lest by establishing their guilt we should afford grounds for
> their death. Rather, they commanded that they stand without communion until
> their time of penance should be fulfilled.

(Presumably the adulteress' husband would become suspicious and kill
her if he saw her performing all the grades of public penance, though
another explanation is that she might be punished by the civil authorities
with death, the penalty for adultery.) So many and so varied are these
cases *not* conforming to the apostasy model that the prudent steward of
souls often must use his own judgment in determining the "economy" of
a penance. Hence Basil the Great, Gregory of Nyssa and other writers on
the subject, after discussing penances in some detail, always end by adding
an appropriate "escape clause." For example:

> If, however, any of those who have been guilty of the aforementioned sins is
> fervent in performing penance, he who by the mercy of God has been entrusted
> with loosing and binding shall not be deserving of censure if, on seeing the
> magnitude of the sinner's penance, he inclines toward clemency and diminishes
> the period of punishment.[8]

Yet there is a further—and far more serious—defect in this approach
to sin and penance. The sins dealt with by the ancient canons are not our
only sins. In his canonical epistles, Basil the Great lays down what is
according to custom in Cappadocia, going back to the days of Firmilian
in his examples. But often by his own counsels whether toward greater
leniency or, at times, toward greater severity, he shows himself opposed to
the legalism of the prevailing system. His own attitude toward penance is
shown more clearly elsewhere in his works. He regrets that his predecessors were so preoccupied with grave sins that they neglected others which

they deemed less serious: wrath, avarice and the like; and he condemns this as "a perverse tradition of men."[9] "I have been rereading the Holy Scriptures," he says, "and I find in the Old Testament as in the New Testament that contumacy against God consists not in the multiplicity or greatness of the sins, but in the violation of any precept whatsoever; the condemnation is the same for any disobedience to God."[10] " ... this distinction between great and little sins doesn't exist in the New Testament. There is but one verdict which pertains to all sins: our Lord saying, 'Everyone who commits sin is a slave to sin' (Jn 8:34). Likewise St John cries out, 'He who does not obey the Son shall not see life, but the wrath of God rests upon him' (3:36). It is not the distinction of sins that gives rise to this threat, but the transgression itself. In a word, if we are permitted to speak of great and little sins, it cannot be denied that the sin is great which masters a person, and small which is mastered by him."[11]

With these words of St Basil, the last drawn from his *Shorter Rule,* we are in quite a different world, the world of monasticism and asceticism, a world of spiritual counsel and direction under the guidance of the *pneumatikos patêr,* a world whose chief theoreticians, beginning with the great Alexandrians Clement and Origen, viewed the essence of the Christian life as gradual purification through spiritual therapy.

Penance in Byzantium

The impact of monasticism, and of its approach to sin and repentance, on the Church's penitential discipline is enormous, perhaps greater than its impact on worship or any other area of the life of the Church. Unfortunately this subject has received comparatively little scholarly attention. Most writers on the history of penance turn directly from antiquity to the western Middle Ages, ignoring crucial developments in the Byzantine East, or else certain extrinsic preconceptions have determined their approach. For example, the interaction of monastic and non-monastic understandings of penance is seen as another chapter in the perpetual struggle of *Geist* and *Amt.* One thing is certain: here, as with penance in antiquity, it is easy to oversimplify, difficult to come up with valid generalizations. Sharp lines of demarcation—until this point, canonical penance; from this point, quasi-monastic confession—cannot be drawn. The influence of the monastic tradition can be felt early. (I think, for example, of the canonical epistle of St Gregory of Nyssa, which tries to harmonize the "seven deadly sins" of monasticism with the older penitential system on the basis of the effect of a given sin on the soul: does it affect the rational, the concupiscible or the irascible part of the soul, or a combination? The artificiality of the approach needs no comment.) At the same time, the older forms of canonical penance survive. It used to be supposed that the abolition of the office of penitentiary priest by Patriarch Nectarius in 391 marked the end of public penance in the Great Church of Constantinople. But in fact public penance survived for centuries, both in Constantinople and elsewhere. The correspondence of Demetrius Chomatianus in the thirteenth century, for example, reveals several such instances.[12]

But if a turning point must be indicated, it certainly would have to be the iconoclastic controversy and its immediate aftermath, when the role of monks as confessors for laymen is for the first time firmly established and systematized. The outlines of this can be seen in the correspondence of St Theodore of Studios[13] and in the penitential canons ascribed (probably falsely) to Patriarch St Nicephorus.[14] The details are provided by the various works ascribed to "John the Faster."[15] These works have nothing to do with the sixth-century patriarch of that name, but neither do they date *ca.* 1100, as some modern scholars have maintained. In fact the oldest form of this farrago of texts, the *Kanonarion,* should be assigned to the early or mid-ninth century, probably to Studite circles.

The chief characteristics of the monastic approach of John the Faster stand in contrast to those of the older system of canonical penance, though with some justice the author constantly interjects, "Not I, but St Basil says ..."

(1) The public aspect of the older system disappears—its various grades, its special dress and the like—and something akin to the early Irish "commutation" is introduced:

> The fact that we reduce the number of years of penance will not, I believe, seem unreasonable to those who are able to reason correctly. For since neither in the writings of our father Basil the Great nor in the more ancient of our venerable fathers has any fasting, vigil or prostration numerically been established for sinners, but simply abstention from holy communion, we have decided that it behooves us, with regard to those who truly repent and desire to subject their flesh to the infliction of hardship and gratefully to lead a life that will counter-

balance their previous wickedness, to counterbalance to them also a reduction of their term of penance in proportion to the measure of their abstinence. For example, if anyone agrees not to drink wine on certain days, we have decided to subtract one year from the sentence established by the fathers for the expiation of his offence. So also, if he promises abstinence from meat for a time, we have seen fit to deduct another year; if from cheese and eggs, or from fish, or from olive oil, etc., for each case of abstinence from any of these products we have seen fit to take off a year. Nor is this all. If he chooses to appease God by frequently repeated prostrations, we have seen fit to do likewise, and especially if he shows a willingness to provide generous alms, without straining his power or overtaxing his ability. If, however, anyone after his fall has entered the God-pleasing solitary life [i.e., monasticism], we have seen fit to shorten still further his sentence, seeing that throughout the rest of his life he is destined to suffer the austerities that befit that way of life.[16]

These penances may be modified yet further to fit the individual:

Son, what are you able to observe? For penances are imposed according to the ability and the preference of those who receive them, and not in proportion to the sins. For it sometimes happens that one who has sinned little, because he is of a generous spirit, accepts his penance willingly and promptly, in order that he may receive not only remission of his sins but even the crown. But one who has sinned much, because he is of a negligent and sluggish spirit, should be punished with little severity, lest he be overwhelmed by the severity of the penance and become discouraged and give up everything.[17]

Above all, these penances are viewed as medicinal, rather than vindicative. The forensic element, present in Western and to an extent in early Christian penitential discipline, disappears beneath a barrage of medicinal imagery. Already the Synod in Trullo (692) presents a concentrated dosage of such language (canon 102):

It is incumbent upon those who have received from God the power to bind and to loose, to consider the quality of the sin and the readiness of the sinner for conversion, and to apply medicine suitable for the disease, lest if he is injudicious in each of these respects he should fail in regard to the healing of the sick man. For the disease of sin is not simple, but various and multiform, and it germinates many mischievous offshoots, from which much evil is diffused, and it proceeds further until it is checked by the power of the physician. Therefore he who professes the science of spiritual medicine first of all should consider the disposition of him who has sinned, and to see whether he tends to health or, on the contrary, provokes his disease by his own behavior, and to look how he can care for his manner of life during the interval. And if he does not resist the physician, and if the ulcer of the soul is increased by the application of the imposed medicaments, then let him mete out mercy to him.[18]

(2) Penances have been modified, and so has procedure. The actual confession of sins, not emphasized in the older system, now comes to the fore. Gentle exploration of spiritual ills on the part of the confessor is facilitated by lists of questions. And foremost among these questions are those dealing with offenses of a sexual nature. If the paradigmatic sin of antiquity was apostasy, that of the Middle Ages is fornication. In the akolouthia for confession ascribed to John the Faster, after the opening psalms and prayers are completed, the confessor first asks: "Tell me, my son, how did you first lose your virginity?"[19] This is quite understandable. The format provided for confession closely follows that for a novice entering upon that life of permanent penance which is monasticism, in which his entire life is reviewed.

(3) A final change raises that perennially popular question of the proper "minister of the sacrament." Who can "forgive sins"? What is the basis for their authority? For Anastasius the Sinaite, the answer was clear: it is the spiritual men, the true "disciples of Christ," the "therapeuts of God," the "stewards of salvation," monks garbed with the robe of repentance who can absolve.[20] St Simeon the New Theologian is even more emphatic: "Before the monks, the bishops alone by succession from the apostles had the power to bind and to loose. But with time the bishops did not use or used badly their power. This redoubtable function ... was then transferred to the elect people of God, that is, the monks."[21] It is above all spiritual gifts that make a confessor, that give him that *parrhêsia* necessary for obtaining forgiveness. Some saints' lives show this very clearly. A Saracen seeks out St Symeon the Stylite to confess that, violating his oath, he had wished to eat meat, and to obtain remission of sins "by the all-powerful prayers of the saint."[22] Another interesting example is related in the acts of the anti-Photian council of 869. A protospatharius named Theodore appears before the legates of the Pope to reply to an accusation against him. When asked whether he has confessed his offense and received a penance, Theodore replies in the affirmative. When the legates ask the name of his confessor, Theodore answers: "I do not know. I know only that he had been a chartophylax, that he was tonsured, and that he had spent forty years on a pillar." The legates ask: "Was he a priest?" Theodore replies: "I do not know. He was an *abba,* and I had faith in the man, and I confessed to him."[23] These cases may be regarded as aberra-

tions, but the same mentality perhaps can be seen in the history of the word *anadokhos*. Originally meaning, "he who goes surety for another," the term is used above all for the sponsor in baptism. By extension, it comes to mean a novice's sponsor for entrance into the monastic life, the elder who hears his first confession, who totally guides and supports him in his spiritual life, who shares in his life of penitence. Finally it frequently comes to refer to the confessor of laymen still living in the world.

The bishop on his throne or the stylite on his pillar: opposition between the two should not be exaggerated. In Byzantium, particularly in the last centuries of the empire, there were always moderating positions. Monks obtain a monopoly in penitential matters, but they must have appropriate letters of commission from the hierarchical authority. For their work, spiritual gifts no doubt are useful, but this above all means "knowing the remedies," knowing what penance to prescribe in a given case, and not some extraordinary psychic powers.[24] St Basil had restricted the task of binding and loosing to "the dispensers of the holy mysteries,"[25] i.e., to priests, and his authority helped to assure that administration of penance for the most part would be restricted to hieromonks. Yet even if the priest is upheld as "the proper minister of the sacrament," this does not mean that the earlier emphasis on the ecclesial context of penance is being affirmed. To monastic claims to special spiritual power are opposed counterclaims to power. Such, for example, is basically the approach of Patriarch St Methodius in dealing with the Studites, who objected to his moderation in dealing with former adherents of iconoclasm and his absolution of the deceased iconoclast Emperor Theophilus. In defending his position, Methodius relies heavily on Pseudo-Dionysius, who henceforth is regularly cited whenever official "economies" are attacked as black magic:

> It is not lawful for a priest to be corrected by those of your rank, O monks, even though he should seem to be unholy in doing divine things or be proved to have done some other forbidden thing... And if judgment is God's, as the Oracles testify, and the priests are angels and interpreters after the bishops of divine judgments, then learn divine things fitting for you, when the time is right, by means of the ministers through whom you were deemed worthy to be a monk.[26]

The ecclesial context of penance has been lost, and with it the eucharistic orientation of the early Church's penitential system. The eucharist is no longer the goal, but simply another tool, like prostrations and fasting, in a program of gradual spiritual improvement. Thus in some of the later texts ascribed to John the Faster, reconciliation to the eucharist becomes only partial. After a certain period of penance, one may receive communion on specified days, like Easter and the Dormition, but in the interval penance must be resumed.[27]

The goal has become "spiritual improvement." But even this is seen in relative terms, just as penances are apportioned according to relative ability. In reading John the Faster, I am reminded of the report cards we had when I was in elementary school: "working up to ability level" was the highest mark awarded. The contrast between this approach and that of antiquity can be seen in a striking way in the course of the tetragamy affair, so called from the uncanonical fourth marriage of Emperor Leo the Wise (906). Writes Patriarch Nicholas Mysticus, castigating Rome for its part in permitting Leo to return to the Church without previous separation from his "wife":

> Is it in the power of Rome so to "economize" that a lawbreaker goes unpunished, and with impure hands lays hold on what is holy? and to lead back into the divine precincts, whence they have been rightly expelled, those who have been driven forth for pollution, even though they have not put their pollution aside? This would be a mighty authority indeed of which you are possessed—an authority possessed not even by Him who "taketh away the sins of the world," let alone by any other, whether of His holy disciples or of the other teachers of the Church! He indeed came to bear our sins, but, naturally, only when we have ceased to sin, not when we are cleaving to and performing without scruple those things which He "taketh away."[28]

Here, as in the early Church, there are certain clear limits to "economy" in penitential matters: the fruits of repentance are demanded. On the other hand Euthymius, Nicholas' successor as patriarch, has no such scruples and admits Leo without demanding separation. After all, that saintly ascetic had been Leo's father confessor. Presumably he knew Leo's spiritual capacities and was willing to take responsibility for him before God. Presumably Leo was "working up to ability level," however low that level might be.

Post-Byzantine Developments

We have seen Byzantium's tendency to turn penance into spiritual guidance under a qualified guru. Let us now turn briefly to the more recent tendency to view confession chiefly as a formal "obligation," whose fulfillment qualifies a person for that other "obligation," reception of the eucharist, and keeps him as a member in good standing in the church community. This too is a complex phenomenon, as little investigated as the interaction of monastic and non-monastic in Byzantium. But "western influence," that all-too-convenient scapegoat for Orthodoxy's difficulties over the last half millennium, is at least in part to blame. Like theological literature, penance undergoes what Fr Georges Florovsky has described as a "pseudomorphosis." Particularly in Russia, it uncritically adopts western forms without really assimilating them. I have already touched upon one aspect of this pseudomorphosis: the change in the formula of absolution from deprecative ("May God forgive ...") to indicative ("I absolve thee ..."). This occurs first in the Vilno *Trebnik* of 1618 and is reproduced virtually unchanged in Peter Moghila's *Trebnik,* along with an explanatory introduction taken directly from Latin instructions on confession published under Pope Paul V in 1603. Because of Moghila's prestige and the clarity of his presentation, this formula became extremely popular, and eventually it was adopted by the whole Russian Church.[29]

This indicative formula of absolution is a fairly obvious example of western influence. But there were other, subtler modifications of the medieval quasi-monastic confessional practice. Among these is the establishment of certain obligatory rules and requirements. In Russia as in Byzantium, specific penitential periods had not originally been prescribed. Only from the seventeenth century were the faithful told that they must go to confession four times a year, during the four fasting seasons, a requirement which was soon reduced to the once-a-year minimum in effect to the present day. (It should come as no surprise to discover that the establishment of these minimum requirements coincides with increased involvement of the civil authorities in religious affairs: annual confession becomes a civil requirement as well as an ecclesiastical one.) At the same time, the relationship of penitent to confessor was given a new legal status. Precise requirements were laid down as to how, where and to whom confession was to be made. By the eighteenth century confession had become so closely regulated that fines were imposed on those not fulfilling the minimum requirements.[30] The monastic tradition's tendency to spiritual individualism gives way, and a juridical element, which in Byzantium had been almost totally obscured by concentration on the medicinal aspect of penance, now comes to the fore. Confession, which in the monastic tradition was seen as one aspect in a comprehensive program for spiritual growth, now is closely linked to membership in the Church. One might even say that in a sense penance is again placed in an ecclesial context, as it had been in Christian antiquity. But with what a difference! For in effect the very definition of the Church has changed. The Church is now understood above all as a horizontal community virtually identical with society as a whole; the vertical element of communion with God in the eucharist is lost from sight. The definition of penance has changed as well. Confession and absolution remain, but too often they are quite removed from any idea of repentance and forgiveness of sins. A striking example is related by Fr Dmitrii Dudko, a priest in Russia today:

> Here's what one priest told me not long ago. A woman came to him for confession. He asked: "How did you sin?" She answered: "I didn't." "Well, then, if you're sinless, you don't need confession. Go on." She didn't leave, but demanded instead that he hear her out. "Listen," she said, "I have a certificate of commendation saying that I have *not* sinned."[31]

With the story of this impeccant woman we have a remarkable example of the gap which can exist in any age between the formal aspects of the Church's penitential discipline and the reality which that discipline should reflect: the reality of sin and of the possibility of repentance and restoration to a life of communion with a loving and forgiving Father, through His Son in the Church established by Him. This example, like many of the others in this survey, perhaps may be dismissed as exaggerated or one-sided, as showing what penitential discipline should *not* be, rather than what it should be in the Orthodox canonical tradition. By using such examples, I have not intended any disrespect for the past. I have tried, however, to avoid absolutizing any one period of church history, to resist the temptation simply to reconstruct the past. The reality of sin, repentance and forgiveness remains. But the ways in which this reality was expressed and conveyed in the third-century Roman Empire—or ninth-century Byzantium or nineteenth-century Russia—are not necessarily the most adequate or appropriate for the twentieth century. Apostasy? Fornication? Is not the besetting sin of our time rather that miserable schizophrenia according to which the Church occupies one compartment of our lives, while all our values and expectations are formed by the increasingly non-Christian world? Lengthy exclusion from communion? Remarkable ascetical practices? Canonists have distinguished vindicative and medicinal penances in the history of canon law. Is this not the time to stress the *educative* aspect of penance? The Orthodox canonical tradition has had a rich and occasionally even colorful past, but what will be its future? Certainly part of our task as Orthodox theologians of the present must be to maintain this tradition as a living and vivifying one, so that "repentance and forgiveness of sins" may be "preached in His name to all nations" more effectively (Lk 24:37).

NOTES

1 Detailed examination in A. Almazov, *Tainaia Ispovied v Pravoslavnoi vostochnoi tserkvi* (Odessa 1894), vol 2.

2 See most conveniently B. Poschmann, *Penance and the Anointing of the Sick* (Herder and Herder, New York 1964; tr from *Busse und Letzte Oelung,* Handbuch der Dogmengeschichte vol 4.3, Herder, Freiburg im Br. 1951) 1-80, and the literature reviewed there.

3 The impact of this model can be seen in a striking way in the penitential ordines of the Armenian, Nestorian and Jacobite rites, which are based ultimately on the ordo for admission to penance of an apostate. Noted by A. Raes, "Les rites de la pénitence chez les Arméniens," *Orientalia Christiana Periodica* 13 (1947) 648-55.

4 Ch. 6, ed and tr R. H. Connolly (Oxford 1929) 40, 52-3.

5 Ch. 10, p 104.

6 Eusebius, *Hist. Eccl.* 7.30.6.

7 These and additional examples in O. D. Watkin's still valuable *History of Penance* (London 1920) vol 1, 327.

8 Basil the Great, canon 74; cf. Gregory of Nyssa canon 5. On use of the word *oikonomia* as a *terminus technicus* in penitential discipline see my article " *Oikonomia* in Byzantine Canon Law," in *Law, Church and Society: Essays in Honor of Stephan Kuttner,* ed K. Pennington and R. Somerville (University of Pennsylvania Press, Philadelphia 1977) 225-36, especially pp 227-9.

9 *De judicio Dei* 7, PG 31, col 669.

10 Ibid. 4, col 661.

11 *Regulae brevius tractatae,* q. 293, PG 31, col 1288.

12 Canon 118, J.-B. Pitra, *Analecta sacra et classica spicilego solesmensi parata,* vol 7 (Paris and Rome 1891) cols 503-6; canon 121, cols 533-6; canon 123, cols 537-8;

canon 144, cols 559-60. From the canons ascribed to Patriarch Nicephorus, 28 and 29 (second recension, PG 100, cols 857-60), it would seem that Byzantium in this period, like the contemporary Carolingian Empire in the West, followed a policy of public fault—public penance, private fault—private penance.

13 Especially *Ep.* 162, PG 99, cols 1504-16.

14 On the various recensions and editions thereof, see H.-G. Beck, *Kirche und theologische Literatur im byzantinischen Reich,* Handbuch der Altertumswissenschaft XII.2.1 (Munich 1959) 490-1.

15 Ed J. Morin, *Commentarius historicus de disciplina in administratione sacramenti poenitentiae* (Paris 1651), appendix. On the text: E. Herman, "Il più antico penitenziale greco," *Orientalia Christiana Periodica* 19 (1953) 70-127.

16 Canon 1 of the 35 canons attributed to John the Faster in the *Pedalion* (Athens 1957) 699.

17 *Akolouthia kai taksis,* ed Morin, appendix p 83.

18 Trans *The Seven Ecumenical Councils,* A Select Library of Nicene and Post-Nicene Fathers, 2nd ser, vol 14, 408.

19 *Akolouthia kai taksis,* ed Morin, appendix p 79.

20 *Quaest. et resp.,* PG 89, cols 369, 372, 373.

21 *Letter on Confession* ch. 11, ed K. Holl, *Enthusiasmus und Bussgewalt beim griechischen Mönchtum* (Leipzig 1898, repr Hildesheim 1969) 120.

22 Theodoret, *Hist. relig.* ch. 26, PG 82, col 1477.

23 J. D. Mansi, *Sacrorum Conciliorum Nova et Amplissima Collectio,* vol 16, cols 150-1. This and the immediately preceding example are noted in the excellent articles s.v. "Confession" in the *Dictionnaire de théologie catholique,* vol 3.1, cols 828-974.

24 Cf. the *entalma* for a spiritual father, PG 119, cols 1152-3.

25 *Regulae brevius tractatae,* q. 288, PG 31, col 1284.

26 *Ep.* 8, To Demophilus, PG 3, col 1088.

27 Cf. *Akolouthia kai taksis,* ed Morin, appendix p 88. The eucharist has become so much a part of the penitential process that reception of communion itself comes to be understood as a form of penance.

28 *Ep.* 32, ed and trans R. J. H. Jenkins and L. G. Westerink, *Nicholas I Patriarch of Constantinople: Letters,* Dumbarton Oaks Texts 2 (Washington 1973) 234-6, slightly modified.

29 Almazov, vol 1, 497-507.

30 Almazov, vol 2, 360-409.

31 *Our Hope* (St Vladimir's Seminary Press, Crestwood, NY 1977) 133-4. Presumably the woman viewed confession above all as a formal obligation to be fulfilled before each reception of the eucharist. On this late development see Almazov, vol 2, 426-35.

Chapter 3

Orthodox Perspectives on Divorce and Remarriage*

The position of the Eastern Orthodox churches on divorce and remarriage is frequently referred to in Western discussions of the subject, but less often is it correctly understood. An older generation of Roman Catholic controversialists regarded the Orthodox as regrettably lax in matters of divorce. More recently those calling for changes in Catholic policies toward the divorced have appealed to the East's more "pastoral approach." Yet seldom have such discussions taken into consideration the very different historical circumstances in which Eastern law and practice developed. As a result, the deepest and most characteristic insights of the Eastern Orthodox have been inadequately explored, while at the same time weaknesses and limitations have been either ignored or misconstrued.

During the Middle Ages, in the course of its own historical development, the Latin Church slowly developed the notion that marriage is essentially a non-voidable contract which, if *ratum* and *consummatum*, persists until the death of one of the partners, remaining by definition indissoluble even if in fact the partners no longer show any signs of being husband and wife. In the words of the new Latin *Code of Canon Law*, "A ratified and consummated marriage cannot be dissolved by any human power or for any reason other than death" (canon 1141). Though even today in the West this understanding of marriage is widely regarded as axiomatic, unchanging and unchangeable, an Eastern Christian, at least in antiquity and in the earlier Middle Ages, would have had difficulty grasping it. For example, he would not have accorded to sexual relations—*a fortiori* to the first sexual act in marriage—a determinative role in the formation of marriage. He also would have had difficulty conceiv-

* Originally presented at the Divorce/Remarriage Symposium, University of Dayton, Dayton OH, March 1989, and published in a collective volume entitled *Divorce and Remarriage* (Sheed and Ward 1990) 17-29.

ing of marriage as such as unconditionally indissoluble. At the same time, he might well have been shocked at the suggestion that Christian marriage is unconditionally dissolved by death, only "till death do us part." How is his apparently contradictory reaction to be explained? A complete answer to this question would require careful examination of the development of marriage doctrine in the Christian East, and above all, the interaction of those components which entered into the development of marriage doctrine in both East and West: Roman law, and Christian tradition as expressed preeminently in Scripture and its interpretation.[1] For an appreciation of the distinctiveness of the Eastern approach, however, and of its possible significance for the issues of divorce and remarriage as they emerge in our own day a thematic approach may prove more fruitful.

"From the Beginning..."

"Have you not read that he who made them from the beginning made them male and female...?" (Mt 19:4). This passage is perhaps the most frequently quoted in Eastern Christian discussions of marriage—quoted more frequently even than Eph 5:32, "This is a great mystery, and I take it to mean Christ and the church." The passage was used, first of all, to defend marriage, established "from the beginning," in paradise before the Fall, against any Marcionite or Encratite disparagement of the essential goodness of creation and sexuality. But, as patristic exegesis of the sequel to these words—"and the two shall become one flesh"—indicates, marriage is not simply divinely sanctioned animality. In the beginning God created them male and female—"co-being," to use the lapidary expression of St Cyril of Alexandria—precisely so that they, in creaturely forms, might reflect and participate in the uncreated life of God the Trinity, a life of perfect openness, of personal communion, of complete sharing, mutual interiority and mutual indwelling.

This is the vocation of marriage "from the beginning," and even after the Fall, something of paradise remains. "When husband and wife cleave to each other in love, there is a remnant of paradise," says Chrysostom.[2] Even after the Fall, after man and woman exchange being for having, true personhood for self-absorbed and self-sufficient individualism, marriage remains their most immediate possibility for transcending autonomous natural necessity through self-giving love. Marriage therefore is not just a remedy against concupiscence, tolerated and legitimized in view of certain natural, utilitarian ends: procreation of children, maintenance of the family and other social institutions. It does not exist to serve the "common good" as distinct from the "particular." When Eastern writers like Chrysostom try to identify and order the aims of marriage, they begin with the "subjective," the nuptial community itself, rather than with the "objective," procreation:

> There are two reasons why marriage was instituted: to make us chaste and to give us children. Of these two reasons, the first takes precedence... especially now that the human race has filled the entire earth. At first the procreation of children was desirable, so that each might leave a memorial of his own life. There was not yet any hope of resurrection, but rather death held sway, and those who died thought that they would perish utterly after this life. Therefore God gave them the comfort of children...But now that the resurrection is at hand, and we do not speak of death but rather advance toward another life better than the present one, the desire for posterity is superfluous.[3]

To be sure, having children does provide obvious opportunities for liberating self-sacrifice, as the fathers noted in their commentaries on I Tim 2:15—"woman will be saved through bearing children." But here too marriage is seen ultimately as a summons to true personal freedom, not just a divinely sanctioned way for perpetuating the species. Like consecrated virginity, to which it is so often compared, marriage "from the beginning" points to the kingdom, where biological bonds and natural affinity are transcended by the immediacy of loving personal relationship.[4]

Interpreted in this eschatological light, Mt 19:4 not only situates the institution and meaning of marriage within the order of creation. It also affirms that perfect and *perpetual* monogamy is the norm of marriage, that for those who believe in the resurrection married love transcends even the necessity of death itself. The second-century apologist Athenagoras sums up what was to remain the widespread feeling of the Christian East: "He who rids himself of his first wife, even if she be dead, is an adulterer in disguise because he transgresses the hand of God, for in the beginning God created but one man and one woman."[5] The Great Church was to distance itself from heretical groups which altogether prohibited remarriage even for widowed spouses. It did not forget that St Paul had even encouraged young widows to remarry. At the same time, remarriage was not held in high esteem. It was a concession to human weakness or natural necessity, not marriage as it had been established "from the beginning," the earthly image of the perfect covenant relationship of God and His people, of Christ and the Church. "Second marriages are not to be condemned," says Epiphanius, "but held in less honor." More pointed is Gregory of Nazianzen: "A first marriage is in full conformity with the law; the second is tolerated by indulgence; the third is noxious. But he who exceeds this number is plainly a swine."[6]

In the East, those entering into second or third marriages were subjected to penance—one or two years for bigamists, up to five years for trigamists according to St Basil the Great, whose "canonical epistles" were incorporated into Eastern canon law collections from the sixth century onward (canon 4). But if, in Basil's words, even a third was not really marriage, but "polygamy, or rather restricted fornication," what of fourth marriage? The Eastern Church rejected forth marriage completely, even though some Christians, like the unfortunate Emperor Leo IV at the beginning of the tenth century, might attempt it. Having lost three wives without issue, he married a fourth time in the hope of gaining a legitimate heir, thus touching off one of the most protracted and bitter disputes in Byzantine history and also the first major quarrel between East and West on marriage matters—for Rome by this point did not scruple successive marriages. The Tome of Union, which ended this "tetragamy affair" and remains even now the last word on the subject for the Eastern Orthodox, utterly prohibited fourth marriage henceforth and allowed third marriage only for those under age forty, with no children from their previous unions—and then with a heavy penance.

"...except for unchastity..."

If in the Eastern Christian tradition Mt 19:4 was the point of departure for reflection on marriage, this text was not considered apart from Mt 19:8-9: The law allowed divorce, "but from the beginning it was not so. And I say to you, whoever divorces his wife except for unchastity (*porneia*), and marries another, commits adultery." The problem of the significance of these words in their Matthean context cannot be examined here. Very possibly Matthew used the exceptive phrase here and in 5:32 having in mind Old Testamental texts like Jer 3:1 (LXX—"If a wife shall be with another man, she shall not return to her husband, but being polluted she remains polluted") and Prov 11:22 (LXX—"He who keeps an adulterous wife is foolish and impious"). In any case, Basil the Great in his "canonical epistles" links Mt 19:9 with these texts and concludes that a man not only may but *must* divorce a wife guilty of *porneia* (canon 9, cf. 21). The same attitude can be seen in canon 8 of the Council of Neocaesarea: a cleric whose wife has committed adultery "must put her away; but if he retain her he can have no part in the ministry committed to him." For the East generally, the Matthean exceptive phrase is understood not as a derogation from the prohibition to divorce but as its logical and necessary corollary. Adultery is the antithesis of marriage as it was established "from the beginning": the perpetual union in love of one man and one woman. In the words of the nineteenth-century Russian lay theologian Alexei Khomiakov, "The holy union instituted by the Creator cannot be dissolved without sin by the human will; but the sin of adultery dissolves it, because adultery is its direct negation. The man who has become just another man in the eyes of his wife, the woman who has become just another woman in the eyes of her husband, are no longer and can no longer be husband and wife in the eyes of the Church."[7] Given this understanding of Mt 19, one can easily understand why an Eastern Christian like Khomiakov would term the Roman concept of indissolubility a "civil servitude." "The idea of organic and mutual union, that is, the inner sanctity of the conjugal state has disappeared."[8]

From the foregoing it is evident that the Eastern Orthodox Church does not just "tolerate" divorce. In some cases it may even counsel it. St John Chrysostom gives an obvious example: "Better to break a marriage for righteousness' sake" than be forced "into some immoral act on the grounds of marriage."[9] Yet as anyone who has experienced the phenomenon of "codependence" can testify, divorce can be as hard as continued "marriage," so strong are the bonds forged by fallen nature. Little wonder that the disciples remark, "If such be the case of a man with his wife, it is not expedient to marry" (Mt 19:10). We are at once reminded that "Not all can receive this saying" (19:11). Byzantine commentators read Mt 19:9 in the light of Mt 5:32, where the prohibition of divorce along with the exceptive clause is set in the course of the Sermon on the Mount. It was seen as an example of Christ's fulfillment of the Law (5:17), of the radical righteousness to which Christ's followers are summoned. It was an ethical demand, a challenge to constant personal struggle against sin, not just as a new and tougher legal prescription.

"...without a valid reason... "

In the event that monogamous marriage was destroyed by the sin of adultery, divorce without remarriage was regarded as the norm for Christians. "Some have made themselves eunuchs for the sake of the kingdom of heaven" (Mt 19:12). Yet this did not altogether exclude the possibility of remarriage—as though "divorce" here meant only separation from bed, board and dwelling but *manente vinculo*, as some Roman Catholic theologians have maintained. In the Byzantine East, heir to the ancient world's concepts and assumptions concerning marriage, the notion of separation as distinct from divorce, or that marriage is by definition indissoluble, remained quite alien for many centuries.

In classical Roman law, marriage was regarded as a factual situation, not as a legal abstraction. It came into existence and continued to exist by the will of partners having the legal capacity for marriage, the *ius connubii*. Withdrawal of the *affectio maritalis* by one or both brought about its dissolution as surely as death did. Divorce whether for serious cause or simply by mutual consent therefore was common in classical times, as was subsequent remarriage.

The early Church did not attempt to replace this civil legal institution with one of its own. "Each of us regards as his the woman whom he married according to your laws," says the apologist Athenagoras.[10] To be sure, the Church did not lose sight of its own standards when dealing with Christians. Thus it apparently was able to see marriage as blessed by God "in the beginning" in the stable, monogamous unions even of those who lacked the *ius connubii* (e.g., slaves) and who therefore were incapable of legal marriage. So also it denounced most forms of divorce as "simply contrary to our laws, even if the Romans judge the matter otherwise."[11] Yet bishops and other churchmen did not question whether divorce and subsequent remarriage was possible by postulating the unconditional indissolubility of matrimony. Patristic and conciliar texts dealing with marriage show signs of hesitation and occasional disharmony, but there is ample evidence of Christians being permitted to remarry after divorce. It is enough to cite the very explicit testimony of St Epiphanius:

> He who cannot keep continence after the death of his first wife or who has separated from his wife for a valid motive, such as fornication, adultery, or some other misdeed, if he takes another wife or if the wife takes another husband, the divine word does not condemn or exclude him from the Church or Life, but rather tolerates this on account of his weakness. Not that this man can keep two wives in his home, the first one still hanging around him. But if he is actually separated from his first wife, he may take another according to the law if this be his desire. [12]

The general direction of the Eastern canonical tradition is clear. While remarriage after divorce is discouraged, just as any remarriage is, restoration to communion without separation from the second spouse is possible not only for the "innocent" party but even for the "guilty," as canon 87 of the Synod in Trullo (692) later provides, though in his or her case only after an appropriately severe penance.

While the establishment of Christianity did not result in a revolution in the Roman law of marriage, there were efforts to check its more objectionable aspects, chief among them being divorce simply by mutual consent. In part this was done by exhortation—as the letters and sermons of churchmen like Basil the Great, Gregory of Nazianzen and John Chrysostom show so clearly. In part it was done by insisting that divorce was unacceptable "without a valid reason" (Trullo canon 87, cf. Basil canons 7, 35, 77). In fits and starts the civil law also tried to limit divorce by tying it to certain specific causes. Justinian in particular was motivated by the idea that "divorce must be the exclusive result of reasonable causes, expressly stated in law"[13]—an idea which was to become a basic principle in later Byzantine jurisprudence. Those divorcing without a valid cause were subject to heavy penalties, at first monetary fines, but under Justinian, compulsory entrance into monasticism. But divorce by mutual consent lingered for centuries, despite the efforts of Justinian and later legislators; and Justinian's attempt (Novella 134) not only to forbid and penalize divorce without valid cause but to decree it null and void was altogether unsuccessful.

The Byzantine "symphony"

The Roman law tradition never died in Byzantium. Indeed, it was self-consciously maintained. But it was slowly transmuted through contact with Christian principles. The Byzantine ideal of "symphony" between *imperium* and *sacerdotium* assumed the concordance of civil law and church law—hence the most characteristic expression of the Byzantine canonical tradition, the *nomocanon,* which conveniently arranged civil *nomoi* and ecclesiastical *kanones* by topic. But if the "conductor" of this Byzantine symphony was the emperor, the melody being played became more and more distinctly Christian. When contradictions between laws and canons were detected, the canons at least in theory took precedence; when the civil laws were revised, passages deemed incompatible with the views of the Church were omitted. In divorce matters the "valid reasons" enumerated by the civil law were reduced to two types: those which could be assimilated to death (disappearance with presumption of death, permanent insanity, monastic habit, episcopal consecration...) and those which could be assimilated to adultery, which thus could be interpreted in the light of the Matthean exceptive clause (endangering the life of the spouse, secret abortion, forcing the spouse to prostitution...), i.e., serious assaults on the moral and spiritual foundations of marriage. At the same time, canonists freely made use of concepts and terminology drawn from Roman law. The Roman jurist Modestinus' definition of marriage as "a union of a man and a woman, and a sharing of the whole of life (*consortium omnis vitae*), a participation in divine and human laws," is repeated again and again in Eastern manuals of theology and canon law down to our own century but developed in a thoroughly Christian direction. The same holds true of Ulpian's dictum that "it is consent and not sexual relations that makes marriage," the emphasis shifting from will to love.[14]

Particularly significant for the later history of marriage in the Christian East were developments touching on the formation of the marital bond. In general the early Church had been more concerned about the character of Christian marriage than about the wedding. In time, diverse non-Christian rituals like crowning were given a Christian interpretation, and wedding festivities were often graced with the presence of Christian priests. Yet this initially had nothing to do with legal requirements. Only in the eighth century is ecclesiastical blessing officially recognized as one of the legal ways for establishing a marriage—and then only as an alternative for the lower classes. But the custom of an ecclesiastical blessing took hold, and in the early tenth century Emperor Leo VI issued his Novella 89:

> ...we order that marriage be confirmed by evidence of a sacred blessing. Therefore, if those who want to get married do not comply with that procedure, from its inception this union shall not be considered as marriage, and such a cohabitation will not produce legal effects.[15]

On the one hand, this decree gave the Church a virtual monopoly in marriage matters. Invested with exclusive responsibility for giving legal status to marriages—and divorces—the Church was able to enforce its own standards much more vigorously than ever before—as Emperor Leo himself would soon find out during the tetragamy affair. At the same time, the distinction between marriages conforming to the Church's norm and those merely tolerated out of condescension to human frailty was blurred. The Church ended up blessing marriages which at least in principle entailed a period of excommunication—the second and third marriages of the widowed and divorced who previously would have had recourse to a civil ceremony. In principle, a distinction was maintained. For example, a separate and distinct Rite of Second Marriage, penitential in tone, was composed. Yet very quickly the rationale for much of the early Church's discipline in marriage matters was forgotten. For example, Neocaesarea canon 7 had forbidden a priest to be present for the wedding banquet of persons entering a second marriage—obviously because this would seem hypocritical in the case of a marriage that entailed excommunication and that could not receive an ecclesiastical blessing. By the twelfth century, however, the commentator Aristenus interprets the canon as meaning that the priest who blesses the marriage cannot attend the reception.[16]

Marriage and Divorce Today

If the surviving accounts of marriage cases are any indication, Byzantine marriage law—that symphony of Roman and Christian elements—functioned reasonably smoothly and effectively. A sign of its strength and resilience may be the fact that it continued to operate without serious problems through most of the Orthodox world after the fall of the Byzantine Empire. Only in our own century has the symphony ended. Intimate links between Church and state, Christianity and society can no longer be taken for granted. The Church is left with the difficult task both of addressing problems unanticipated in the old nomocanonic system and of modifying elements in it which have in fact become dysfunctional. Confronted with this new situation, the Church faces many temptations. Instead of communicating its own deepest insights about marriage to the world of today, it could end up woodenly maintaining all the external forms and requirements of a bygone age, whether civil or ecclesiastical, and in the very process capitulate to an understanding of marriage quite at odds with Christian teaching.

Part of the present difficulty can be traced to the Byzantine require-ment that a marriage must receive a priestly blessing in order to be valid. As in the Latin Church after Trent, attention in matrimonial cases tended to shift from the content of Christian marriage to the required form, from the capacity and commitment of the couple themselves to external ele-ments which can be more easily introduced as evidence in a court of law. Complicating the Eastern situation further was the influence of Western scholastic principles of sacramental theology from the thirteenth century onward. Marriage is fitted rather awkwardly into the system of seven sacraments, and its proper minister is identified: but as the priest, and not—as the Latins maintained —the couple themselves.

It is understandable why, in the unitary Byzantine and post-Byzantine world, avoidance of ecclesiastical blessing could be regarded as tanta-mount to rejection of Christian teaching on marriage. But in the pluralis-tic world of the twentieth century, can we seriously maintain that marriages blessed by an Orthodox priest in the Orthodox Church accord-ing to the Orthodox Rite of Matrimony necessarily "count," while those not so blessed do not? Yet this what some of the Orthodox churches today attempt to do. Converts to Orthodoxy are encouraged—or even re-quired—to be remarried in a church wedding. Men married, divorced and remarried anywhere "outside" the Orthodox Church may become candidates for ordination because the impediment of sequential bigamy, which traditionally has been taken very seriously by the Orthodoxy, is not considered to be present in their case. The list of anomalies could go on and on. To be sure, other Orthodox churches—most notably the Russian—take quite a different approach. For example, they grant dispensations from form in certain cases, and they "count" marriages entered into "outside" the Church provided that the qualities which the Church requires of marriage are present. That such widely divergent practices can exist among the Orthodox churches suggests how confused the Orthodox understanding of marriage has become since the end of the Byzantine symphony.

Many other contemporary problems could be enumerated. How, for example, are the marriages of persons who in fact are non-religious agnostics to be regarded, even though these may have been blessed by an Orthodox priest in the Orthodox Church according to the Orthodox Rite of Matrimony? Or what consideration should be given to psychological factors which might adversely affect a couple's capacity to relate to each other as husband and wife? The nomocanonic system allowed divorce but virtually ignored the concept of nullity. In these and many other areas, deeper reflection is urgently needed.

In his massive study of *Divorce and Remarriage*, Fr Theodore Mackin observes that a chief concern of the fathers of the early Church "was to get Christian spouses to see their marriage not as liasons become marriages sanctioned by Roman law, but as relationships of respect and caring love designed by God."[17] In our post-Christian age we face much the same challenge, save that now our own ecclesiastical forms may be among the obstacles which hinder a deeper understanding of Christian marriage. Fortunately the Orthodox tradition does offer many resources for this task: a firm but sensitive understanding of penitential discipline, a history of liturgical creativity, a tradition of openness to culture and to the problems of society, an approach to the sacraments not entirely imprisoned in scholastic theories, a pastoral theology solidly grounded in dogmatic theology, stressing the ultimate significance of personhood... Our greatest challenge may simply be in allowing these resources to become more than reminders of a glorious past and applying them to the needs of our own time and place.

NOTES

1 See N. van der Wal, "Secular Law and the Eastern Church's Concept of Marriage," *Concilium* 5.6 (London, May 1970) 76-82; O. Rousseau, "Divorce and Remarriage: East and West," *Concilium* 24 (New York, April 1967) 119-38; J. Dauvillier and C. de Clerq, *Le mariage en droit canonique oriental* (Paris 1936); and especially the very erudite recent studies of Abp Peter (Pierre) L'Huillier, "The Indissolubility of Marriage in Orthodox Law and Practice," *St Vladimir's Theological Quarterly* 32 (1988) 199-221, "L'attitude de l'Eglise Orthodoxe vis-à-vis du remarriage des divorces," *Revue de Droit Canonique* 29 (1979) 44-59, and "Novella 89 of Leo the Wise on Marriage: An Insight into its Theoretical and Practical Impact," *Greek Orthodox Theological Review* 32 (1987) 153-62.

2 Hom. 20, on the writ of divorce, PG 51, col 221.

3 Hom. 19, on marriage, PG 51, col 213.

4 Among modern recent Orthodox writers on these themes see especially P. Evdokimov, *The Sacrament of Love* (St Vladimir's Seminary Press, Crestwood, NY 1985); C. Yannaras, *The Freedom of Morality* (St Vladimir's Seminary Press, Crestwood, NY 1984) 157-72; and also the studies of J. Meyendorff, *Marriage: An Orthodox Perspective* (St Vladimir's Seminary Press, Crestwood, NY 1975) and T. Stylianopoulos, "Toward a Theology of Marriage in the Orthodox Church," *Greek Orthodox Theological Review* 22 (1977) 249-83.

5 *Supplication* 33, PG 6, col 968.

6 *Or.* 37.8, PG 36, col 292.

7 *L'Eglise Latine et le Protestantisme au point de vue de l'Eglise d'Orient* (Lausanne 1872) 154.

8 Ibid. Cf. the comments of Evdokimov, p 188: "A person who betrays his love betrays himself. But this need to remain on the level of the spirit can never be formalized or decreed. Love, like martyrdom, cannot be imposed on someone. The promise of fidelity is borne on the deepest realities of human life and on transactional realities. It is not imposed from without but raised from within, from the heart's dimension, and is addressed to the freedom of the spirit like an invitation to a banquet and a call to suffering. The act of faith enters into it, and one's fidelity comes alive in accordance with the integrity of one's faith. Within this mystery no one is judge except God, to whom the promise is made, and the conscience of the one who made the promise. If faith changes, fidelity also changes; it ceases to be a grace and it becomes a constraint." Evdokimov sums up the Orthodox position in this way (p 189): "In permitting divorce, the Orthodox Church shows its infinite respect for the person and for the sacrament of charismatic love."

9 Hom. 19 on 1 Cor, PG 61, col 155.

10 *Supplication* 33, PG 6, col 968.

11 Gregory of Nazianzen, *Ep.* 144, PG 37, col 248.

12 *Panarion*, heresy 59, PG 41, col 1025.

13 L'Huillier, "Indissolubility," 209.

14 Cf. the understanding of marriage set forth in Vatican II's *Gaudium et Spes*. Marriage is referred to as "the intimate partnership of life and love...an intimate union...a mutual giving of two persons" (48). "Married love...is an affection between two persons rooted in the will and it embraces the good of the whole person... A love like that, bringing together the human and the divine, leads the partners to free and mutual giving of self, experienced in tenderness and action, and penetrates their whole lives" (49). Here again, the Roman law conception of marriage has been thoroughly imbued with Christian values. This understanding of marriage has important implications not only for marriage jurisprudence within the Roman communion (on which see especially T. Mackin, *What is Marriage?* [Paulist Press, New York/Ramsey 1982] pp 283-327) but also for ecumenical relations.

15 P. Noailles and A. Dain, *Les Novelles de Leon VI le Sage* (Paris 1944) 297, trans L'Huillier, "Novella 89," 158.

16 Noted by L'Huillier, "Novella 89," 160-61.

17 Paulist Press, New York (Ramsey 1984) 150.

Chapter 4

The Priesthood in Patristic Teaching*

To speak of "the *priesthood* in patristic teaching"—or "in the canons," or "in the liturgical tradition," or whatever—perhaps is inevitable, but it is also misleading. It may be inevitable given the historical trajectory of our terminology for ministry, but it is misleading if as a result our understanding of ministry is reduced to narrowly cultic terms.[1]

As the New Testament indicates, the Church from its earliest days has known an official ministry: certain ones whom "God has appointed in the Church, first apostles, second prophets, third teachers..." (I Cor 12:28); "overseers and deacons" (Phil 1:1); "elders...appointed in every church" (Acts 14:23); persons who labor among the brethren, who are over them in the Lord and who admonish them, who therefore are due respect and high esteem (I Thess 5:12-3). To be sure, this ministry is not described as priesthood. As is well known, the New Testament uses that term sparingly, in reference to the temple cultus of the old covenant, in reference to Christ Himself (see especially Hebrews) and in reference to the Christian people of God (I Pet, Rev). But by the end of the first or the early second century the official ministry of the Church does come to be referred to in priestly, cultic terms: The *Didachê* (15:1-2) calls its itinerant prophets (whose specific liturgy involved giving thanks at the eucharist) "high priests"; Ignatius speaks of the "one altar" of the eucharist at which the bishop presides (*Magn.* 7:2); *I Clement* refers to bishops as persons who "have offered the sacrifices" (44:4) and argues that proper order in the Church is analogous to the ministry of the temple, with its distinctions between high priest, priests, levites and laity (40:5). By the end of the second and the early third century, in the age of Hippolytus and Tertul-

* Originally presented at the Inter-Orthodox Theological Consultation on the Place of the Woman in the Orthodox Church and the Question of the Ordination of Women, Rhodos, Greece, October 30-November 7, 1988.

lian, the bishop can be called *archiereus/sacerdos* and his ministry described
as sacerdotal; and in time this vocabulary comes to be extended, apparently by association, to the bishop's colleagues in ministry. Presbyters,
according to Cyprian, are "associated with the bishop in the honor of
priesthood" (*Ep.* 61:3); according to Innocent I, they are "priests of the
second degree" (*Ep.* 25:3). Leo the Great on one occasion even includes
the bishop's assistants, the deacons, in the priestly *ordo* (*Ep.* 6:6); and in
the East at least one writer, St Epiphanius, extends the priestly hierarchy
(*hê hierosunê*) to include subdeacons as well.[2] Priesthood, in short, appears to be on its way to becoming a generic term for clergy, the *sacerdotium* of the medieval West. The term comes to suggest an autonomous
power to perform certain sacred acts—above all to make bread and wine
the body and blood of Christ—which is transmitted from ordainer to
ordained without necessary reference to ecclesial context and which all
too easily is considered quite apart from trinitarian theology or even from
a sound christology.

Such a reduction is altogether alien to patristic thought, however. For
the fathers, the vocabulary of priesthood is used not so much to denote a
particular order or office as to call attention to a particular aspect of the
church's ministry of pastoral leadership.[3] The fathers maintain and indeed
expand the New Testament's rich vocabulary for official ministry. As a
result, the term "priesthood" is qualified and conditioned by a variety of
other terms. The "priest" is not only *hiereus* but also *proestos* or *proistamenos, proedros, hegoumenos, didaskalos, mystagôgos, iatros tôn psychôn,
oikonomos tôn mysteriôn...* These mutually qualifying, but also mutually
reinforcing designations alert us first of all to the danger of viewing
Christian priesthood simply as another version of that cultic, ritual priesthood which has existed in so many human societies and religions (e.g. the
mystery religions of the Hellenistic world). Quite simply, the Christian
priest does not function authentically in the same way as does a priest or
priestess or shaman in other world religions, just as he does not "lead" in
the same way that various "leaders" of twentieth-century sociopolitical
systems lead, or "rule" in the same way that princes or potentates rule, or
"manage" in the same way that well-trained modern chief executive
officers manage.[4] Authentic Christian priesthood can be defined only by
reference to its role within the Christian Church, and this in turn can be

understood only by reference to the entire economy of salvation: the mystery of God's hidden plan for humankind revealed in Jesus Christ and communicated through the Holy Spirit.

Before we explore patristic thought on this subject, a few comments concerning methodology may be in order. The fathers did not develop a comprehensive and systematic, much less a uniform doctrine of the priesthood or indeed of the Church. (Thus it may be misleading to speak of "the priesthood in patristic *teaching*," if by this term we are led to expect monolithic uniformity.) In the West there was some movement in this direction, most notably with Augustine's response to Donatism; but in the East the challenge of heresy, which conditioned and set the direction for the formulation of trinitarian and christological dogma, was relatively insignificant in the realm of ecclesiology. The fathers' teaching on the priesthood developed in different circumstances. With some, remarkably profound thought on the subject can be inferred from comments and expressions scattered throughout their writings. This is certainly the case with St Basil.[5] Others, notably St Gregory of Nazianzen and St John Chrysostom in the East, directly addressed the subject of the priesthood, characteristically in the form of apologia setting forth the awesome responsibilities and duties of the priestly ministry while at the same time protesting their own unworthiness for this ministry. Such works, along with the manuals of church order which flourished particularly in Syria in this period, are not systematic doctrinal presentations. Rather, they offer theological reflections on the priestly ministry which take as their point of departure the actual practice of this ministry. Given the varied and occasional nature of our sources, the high level of agreement and coherence which we in fact find is all the more remarkable. I believe, therefore, that we can properly speak of "patristic teaching" on the priesthood. In reading the fathers on this subject we are confronted, not by a disparate collection of theological opinions formed on the basis of this or that philosophical *a priori* or polemical concern but rather a coherent expression of the very life of the Church.

The *Didascalia Apostolorum*, which devotes five full chapters to the episcopal office, provides an early example of such theological reflection on pastoral practice. Clergy and laity together comprise "the Catholic Church, the holy and perfect, a royal priesthood, a holy multitude, a people for inheritance,"[6] within which the bishops are "priests and prophets, and princes and leaders and kings, and mediators between God and the faithful, and receivers of the word, and preachers and proclaimers therof, and knowers of the Scriptures and of the utterances of God, and witnesses of his will, who bear the sins of all, and are to give answer for all"[7]—note the breadth of this definition! The bishop's office is indeed lofty, so that "the layman loves the bishop and honors and fears him as father and lord and God after God almighty." At the same time, we are reminded that the priest/bishop must be "without blemish in the things of this world, and likewise in his body."[8] We find a twofold emphasis, which runs throughout the patristic tradition: emphasis on the dignity and authority of priesthood and at the same time on the moral and spiritual requirements for it.

Pursuing many of the same themes, St Gregory of Nazianzen puts priesthood firmly in its place within the history of salvation. The whole purpose of God's plan, he affirms, is the restoration of the divine image in man, and in this we here and now "are the ministers (*hyperetai*) and fellow-workers (*synergoi*)—all we who preside over (*prokathezometha*) others."[9] "The whole aim of our art is to give wings to the soul, to wean it from the world and to present it to God; to preserve the image of God in man if it exists, to strengthen it if it has become enfeebled, and to restore it if it has become obliterated; to make Christ dwell in men's hearts through the Spirit. In a word, the aim is to deify and bestow the blessedness of heaven upon him who in fact belongs to heaven."[10] The priest "restores the creature, he reveals the image, he works for the heavenly world and, greatest of all, he is a god who fashions gods."[11] He is the instrument of a work which is, properly speaking, divine: the deification of man. Yet in this work he is *synergos*, collaborator with God. The priest participates in God's hidden plan for humankind, and in so doing he not only transforms but is himself transformed.[12]

Theosis and *synergeia*, deification and cooperation: Here we approach the very heart of the Greek fathers' teaching on the priesthood, which is the heart as well of their teaching on spirituality. Viewed from one perspective, the priest is only an instrument. St John Chrysostom expresses this very forcefully, in terms that challenge some of our preconceived notions of Antiochian "anthropological maximalism" (Florovsky).

"Do you not know what the priest (*hiereus*) is? He is an angel from the Lord. Are his words his own? If you despise him, it is not him you despise but God who ordained (*kheirotonêsantos*) him. If God does not work through him, then there is no more baptism or communion in the mysteries..."[13] The honor and authority of the priesthood depends on God, not man, so that even an unworthy priest remains an instrument of his saving activity: "Is he unworthy? How does that affect the matter? God has indeed made use of oxen to save His people. It is not the life of the priest or his virtues which accomplish such a thing. Everything springs from grace. The priest has but to open his mouth, for it is God who effects everything. The priest only performs the sign (*symbolon*). The oblation is the same no matter who offers it, whether Peter or Paul. One is no less than the other, for it is not men who consecrate (*hagiazousi*) it, but God Himself who bestows sanctification."[14]

Here we seem very close indeed to Augustine's emphasis, against the Donatists, on the primacy of grace. Yet for Chrysostom and the East generally, this does not lead to an exaggerated emphasis on the effectiveness of the sacraments *ex opere operato* and in turn to a reliance simply on institutional authority. God's work of deification does not suppress human freedom and responsibility or make it of no account. Just as the *Didascalia Apostolorum* earlier, Chrysostom emphasizes the moral and spiritual requirements of the priesthood, often in the same breath as he calls attention to its dignity and authority: "The work of the priesthood is done on earth, but it is ranked among heavenly ordinances. And this is only right, for no angel, no archangel, no other created power, but the Paraclete himself ordained this succession and persuaded men while still remaining in the flesh to represent the ministry of angels. The priest, therefore, must be as pure as if he were standing in heaven itself, in the midst of those powers."[15] In much the same tone St Gregory of Nazianzen writes: "...before a man has, as far as possible, sufficiently purified his mind and far surpassed his fellows in nearness to God, I do not think it safe for him to be entrusted with the rule over souls or the office of mediator...between God and man."[16]

Is there any way in which we can explicate this mystery of divine action and human response without reducing one of its terms to insignificance, without becoming either Pelagians, reliant on our own human works, or else spiritual and ecclesiological Monophysites, altogether passive before the divine initiative? The full scope of this question obviously cannot be explored here, yet at least one point—obvious but fundamental—must be noted: the prominence of the pneumatological element in Orthodox ecclesiology and sacramental theology, with their emphasis on the role of the Holy Spirit both as distributer of spiritual gifts and as the one who brings them all into harmonious unity in the Church. If, as is frequently noted, the Eastern fathers refuse to distinguish sharply between the "institutional" and the "charismatic," surely this is above all because of their understanding of the Holy Spirit.[17] On the one hand, this means that the charismata of leadership, knowledge, teaching, sanctity are not merely subjective attainments of individuals—this would indeed be Pelagianism. Rather they are revealed truly as gifts of the Spirit only when they are exercised within and for the Church. But at the same time, priestly ministry is inconceivable without these gifts, for without the Spirit and His manifold gifts—without the personal experience of God which is possible only in the Spirit—the Church with its official ministry would not just become "institutional": it would cease to be the Church. The Church—and her ministry—therefore lives in a continuous state of invocation, of *epiklēsis*, awaiting the pentecostal Spirit "who provides all things, who fulfills the priesthood, who has taught wisdom to the illiterate, revealing fishermen as theologians and bringing together all the laws of the Church" (Vespers of Pentecost, third sticheron).

If we look more closely at the various functions or aspects of the priestly ministry—teaching, governing, sanctifying—as these are set forth in patristic literature, we again see the impossibility of opposing "spirit" to "office," "charismatic authority" to "institutional authority." This is especially true if we consider the priest's ministry of the word, the work of evangelizing and converting, teaching and reproving. Already St Paul seems to have given this ministry preeminent dignity: "Christ sent me, not to baptize but to preach the gospel" (1 Cor 1:17). This emphasis continues particularly in the Alexandrian tradition with Origen, but it can be found throughout patristic literature. Chrysostom, for example, devotes roughly two of his six books on the priesthood to this subject, and Gregory of Nazianzen can write: "We come now to the dispensation of the word, so that in last and most important place we might speak of what comes first in our ministry."[18] On the one hand, this ministry is distinctly priestly. It depends not so much on human reasoning or learning as on the divine Word itself. "Proclaiming the gospel is priestly work," writes Origen.[19] It is for this reason that he can see the continuation of the Old Testamental priesthood precisely in the new covenant's ministry of the word: "When you see that the priests and levites are no longer handling the blood of rams and bulls, but the Word of God by the grace of the Holy Spirit, then you can say that Jesus has taken the place of Moses."[20] Yet human beings charged with the ministry of the word must be endowed with gifts of the Spirit. Origen, the intellectual, stresses the gift of learning. A more holistic approach is taken by Chrysostom, who regularly emphasizes the good judgment and tact demanded of the preacher/teacher, and by Gregory of Nazianzen, who insists on the need "to give in due season to each his portion of the word."[21] The goal of the minister of the word is not just to convey information but to raise the soul to a transforming knowledge of God through entry into the mystery of the divine dispensation, through participation in God's saving plan for humankind. For this reason, "since the common body of the Church is composed of many different characters and minds... , it is absolutely necessary that its ruler should be at once simple in his uprightness... , and as far as possible manifold and varied in his treatment of individuals..."[22] The spiritual gift of discernment and a proper sense of "economy" are essential for the exercise of the Church's "teaching office."

Also "charismatic" is another aspect of the priestly ministry which too easily is marginalized or divorced from its other aspects: the ministry of leading, ruling, presiding, administering. Among the charismatics Paul numbers *ho proistamenos,* "the one who rules" (Rom 12:8). The *Didascalia Apostolorum* refers to priests as "princes and leaders and kings" in the same breath as it refers to them as "prophets," and it spends considerable time exhorting "the good stewards of God" to "dispense well" the things which they have been given, "to the orphans, the widows, the needy and the strangers."[23] In all such activities, as Chrysostom notes, the priest must possess not only financial acumen and integrity but also "forbearance, the source of all human blessings, which guides the soul to anchorage and escorts it into a fair haven."[24] Here again, the work done by the priest is properly the work of God, and for its accomplishment spiritual gifts, not simply mundane talents, are needed.

Of course the most obvious aspect of the priest's ministry, particularly for us today, is liturgical. He is the "minister of the sacraments," above all of the eucharist. Here especially, the human, synergic element tends to recede from our sight: the works done at the hands of the priest are manifestly divine. The fathers also marvel at this awesome wonder. Chrysostom exclaims: "When you see the Lord sacrificed and lying before you, and the High Priest standing over the sacrifice and praying, and all who partake being tinctured with that precious blood, can you think that you are still among men and still standing on earth? Are you not at once transported to heaven...?"[25] Yet the call to human cooperation is never altogether absent. As St Gregory of Nazianzen declares in the course of his discussion of the majesty of the priest's eucharistic ministry, "no one is worthy of the mightiness of God, and the sacrifice, and the priesthood, who has not first presented himself to God, a living, holy sacrifice."[26]

Here we should also note that the fathers' discussion of the priest's liturgical and sacramental ministry is by no means limited to the eucharist. Chrysostom, for example, gives equal if not greater prominence to the fact that priests "are the ones—they and no others—who are in charge of spiritual travail and responsible for the birth that comes through baptism." It is for this reason, he argues, that they should be "more honored even than parents. For our parents begot us 'of blood and the will of the flesh,' but they are responsible for our birth from God, that blessed second birth, our true emancipation, the adoption according to grace."[27] Yet perhaps greatest of all is the priests' authority "not over leprosy of the body but over uncleanness of the soul, and not just to certify its cure, but actually to cure it," the authority "to remit sins, not only when they make us regenerate, but afterwards too."[28] Whether we look at the classic patristic treatises on the pastoral office or at manuals like the *Didascalia Apostolorum*, particular emphasis is given to the role of the priest as minister of forgiveness. This activity involves judgment and admonition, as the *Didascalia Apostolorum* stresses. But it is above all a healing art to which—as St Gregory Nazianzen particularly emphasizes—the diverse other aspects of priestly ministry must be brought to bear: teaching—above all by "training people in an entire way of life"—and ruling—above all by "the influence of persuasion."[29] Here again, the central themes of patristic spirituality—divine action and human collaboration—emerge as central themes in the patristic understanding of the priesthood.

Our survey of "the priesthood in patristic teaching" could well end at this point were it not for the fact that the express purpose of this consultation is to consider "the place of women in the Orthodox Church and the question of the ordination of women." Our recent preoccupation with the question of women's ordination was not shared by the fathers, who for the most part simply take it for granted that a woman cannot exercise the ministry of priesthood and who consequently do not systematically analyze the question.

A noteworthy exception is St Epiphanius, who in his account of various heretical groups examines the possibility of women priests at length. He appeals specifically to the praxis of Christ, the apostles and the Church throughout the ages: "Never since the beginning of time has a woman served God as priest."[30] "God never appointed to this ministry a single woman upon earth,"[31] not even Mary, "though from her womb and her bosom she took the king of all men, the heavenly God, the Son of God."[32] As Bishop Kallistos Ware remarks, "Most Orthodox today would find Epiphanius' treatment of the subject both convincing and sufficient. The ordination of women to the priesthood is an innovation, with no sound basis whatsoever in Holy Tradition." But as he immediately goes on to add, "It has to be admitted, however, that this argument for tradition will seem inadequate to the majority of Christians in the West, even to many who are themselves opposed to the ordination of women as priests. It is not enough for them to be told that it is not in tradition; they wish to know why it is not."[33]

Do the fathers offer any hint of an answer to this question? Here it may be appropriate first to note one line of argumentation which they do *not* develop: the argument that in the exercise of his official functions—and above all in the eucharist—the priest directly represents Christ, that he acts *in persona Christi* "to the point of being his very image," so that "natural resemblance" to Christ—including masculinity—is a prerequisite for ordination. This argument, here summarized from *Inter Insigniores*, the Sacred Congregation for the Doctrine of the Faith's *Declaration on the Question of the Admission of Women to the Ministerial Priesthood*, can also be found in several modern Orthodox discussions of the subject. In certain respects, however, it runs directly counter to the patristic teaching on the priesthood which we have been exploring thus far. (1) This argument, first of all, focuses almost exclusively on the priest as celebrant of the eucharist, neglecting the many other aspects of the priestly ministry which the fathers develop with such sensitivity. (2) Moreover the argument, especially as it is developed in *Inter Insigniores*, presupposes one particular doctrine of the eucharist which locates the "moment of consecration" at the point when the priest repeats the dominical words of institution.[34] By emphasizing the intervention of Christ present to His Church in the person of the celebrant, this doctrine underscores the "divine action" to which I have referred so many times, but it does so at the expense of the epicletic element which—as I have also argued—is altogether crucial for the Orthodox understanding of the Church and its priestly ministry. In effect, the doctrine suggests that there can exist an institutional representation of Christ which functions independently of the Church formed by the Holy Spirit into one body and filled with His gifts, whereas patristic teaching tries to hold together "spirit" and "office," "charismatic authority" and "institutional authority." (3) Finally, the argument from "natural resemblance" finds little resonance in the fathers, who are more concerned about the priest's internal and ethical conformity to Christ than they are with his external and physical conformity. When, for example, they refer to the "wholeness" and other qualities demanded of the levitical priesthood, they regularly contrast the carnal meaning which these had in the Old Testament, with the spiritual meaning which they now have in the new covenant.[35]

More in harmony with the teaching of many of the fathers, most notably of St John Chrysostom, are arguments that stress the headship of the male (see especially patristic commentaries on 1 Cor 11:3, 1 Cor 14:34-5, Titus 2:3-4 and 1 Tim 2:12 and such texts as the *Apostolic Constitutions* 3.9.14): The unchanging order of creation has established a diversity of role and function for the two sexes that permits the exercise of leadership and authority in the Church to males only. It must be acknowledged, however, that patristic attitudes on this subject may have been molded by contemporary legal and social conventions as much as by Christian revelation. Consider, for example, this passage from "Ambrosiaster": "It is obvious that woman is submitted to man's power and that she does not have authority. For she can neither teach, nor be a witness, nor give guarantees, nor administer justice, and so, how much less is she than capable of exercising power."[36] The author explains woman's incapacity for the exercise of authority by appealing entirely to examples drawn from contemporary Roman law—a law which he no doubt saw as simply reflecting the law of nature. In our day very few—even those most outspoken in their opposition to the ordination of women—would so radically exclude women from all positions of responsibility in secular society. Yet if the order of creation excludes women from positions of leadership and authority, surely this should apply to positions in society as well as to positions in the Church. Here again we see the hazards of appealing too quickly to patristic testimony. We must admit quite simply: while the fathers have blessed us with a multifaceted yet coherent teaching on the priesthood, they have not given us a complete and altogether satisfactory answer to the question of the ordination of women.

NOTES

1 On our subject see most conveniently R. A. Norris, "The Beginnings of Christian Priesthood," *Anglican Theological Review* 66, supplementary series #9 (1984) 18-32; T. J. Talley, "The Liturgical Role of the Bishop," *Worship* 42 (1968) 2-13; J. Daniélou, "The Priestly Ministry in the Greek Fathers," and P. M. Gy, "Notes on the Early Terminology of Christian Priesthood," in *The Sacrament of Holy Orders* (= proceedings of the 1955 session of the Centre de Pastorale Liturgique; Liturgical Press, Collegeville, MN 1962) 116-26 and 98-115 respectively; and, from a distinctly Protestant perspective, H. von Campenhausen, "The Origins of the Idea of the Priesthood in the Early Church," in *Tradition and Life in the Church: Essays and Lectures in Church History* (Fortress Press, Philadelphia 1968) 217-30.

2 *Panarion* 3:2, Exp. 21; PG 42, col 821-5.

3 Cf. Norris, p 19.

4 Cf. the remarks of A. Kavanagh in his penetrating essay on "Christian Ministry and Ministries," *Anglican Theological Review* 66, supplementary series #9 (1984) 36-48 at p 39.

5 See the outstanding study of P. J. Fedwick, *The Church and the Charisma of Leadership in Basil of Caesarea* (Pontifical Institute of Medieval Studies, Toronto 1979).

6 Ed Connolly (Oxford 1929) p 86.

7 P 80.

8 P 32; cf. Lev 21:17.

9 *Apol.* 26; PG 35, col 436.

10 Ibid. 22; PG 35, col 432.

11 Ibid. 73; PG 35, col 481.

12 On this theme and what follows see especially the presentation of Daniélou, pp 119-21.

13 *Hom. on II Tim. 1,* 2:3; PG 62, col 610.

14 Ibid. 2:4; 612.

15 *Priesthood* 3:4; PG 48, col 642.

16 *Apol.* 91; PG 35, col 493.

17 Cf. J. Zizioulas, "Ministry and Communion," in his *Being as Communion* (St Vladimir's Seminary Press, Crestwood, NY 1985) pp 209-46.

18 *Apol.* 35; PG 35, col 444.

19 *Com. on Rom.* 10:2; PG 14, col 1252.

20 *Hom. on Jos.* 2:1; Sources Chrétiennes 71, pp 116-17.

21 *Apol.* 35; PG 35, col 444.

22 *Apol.* 44; PG 35, col 452-3.

23 Ed Connolly, p 80.

24 *Priesthood* 3:16; PG 48, col 656.

25 *Priesthood* 3:4; PG 48, col 642.

26 *Apol.* 95; PG 35, col 497.

27 *Priesthood* 3:5; PG 48, col 644.

28 Ibid. 3:6; PG 48, col 646.

29 *Apol.* 15; PG 35, col 424.

30 *Panarion* 3:2, heresy 79:2; PG 42, col 741.

31 Ibid. 79:7; PG 42, col 752.

32 Ibid. 79:3; PG 42, col 744.

33 "Man, Woman and the Priesthood of Christ," in *Women and the Priesthood* (ed T. Hopko, St Vladimir's Seminary Press, Crestwood, NY 1983) 9-37 at p 19.

34 On this subject see especially the critique given in the research report commissioned by the Catholic Theological Society of America on *Women in Church and Society* (ed S. Butler, 1978) 25-32.

35 Cf. also the provisions of Apostolic Canons 21 and 22, of I Nicea canon 1 concerning eunuchs, and the provisions of Apostolic Canons 77 and 78 concerning the physically handicapped: "If anyone be deprived of an eye or lame of a leg but in other respects be worth of a bishopric, he may be ordained, for the defect of the body does not defile a man, but the pollution of the soul. But if a man be deaf or blind, he may not be made a bishop, not indeed as if he were thus defiled, but that the affairs of the Church may not be hindered."

36 Corpus Scriptorum Ecclesiasticorum Latinorum 50, 82.14-83.15.

Chapter 5

Eucharist and Ministry in Ecumenical Dialogue*

Eucharist and ministry: the conjunction of these terms in recent ecumenical discussion suggests a relationship to be explored. Eucharist and ministry are not treated as isolated items haphazardly selected from a longer list of topics for debate. Rather, both are placed in a broader ecclesial perspective in which the Church's structures are seen as arising from and as intimately linked to the Church's life of faith, and the Church's life of faith is seen not in individualistic or totally "spiritualized" terms, but above all as the corporate life of the faithful gathered as Christ's body in the eucharist.

The Ecclesial Significance of the Eucharist

Until recently discussion of the eucharist—like that of so many other divisive issues—has most often been determined by categories of thought inherited from the Latin Middle Ages. From the twelfth century the *corpus Christi mysticum* (i.e., the Church) and the *corpus Christi eucharisticum*—once radically identified with one another—came to be distinguished ever more sharply. The Church came to be understood above all as a divinely instituted, hierarchically ordered body politic, and the eucharist, one of several "means of grace" dispensed by it for the spiritual growth of individual members. The Reformation challenged medieval teaching on the eucharist at several specific points: the mode of Christ's presence in the eucharist was reinterpreted, the sacrificial nature of the eucharist was questioned ... Yet just as before, the eucharist was regarded chiefly as indicating what the Church does, not what the Church is. It was one of the Church's "corporate forms of worship";[1] and

* Originally published in *St Vladimir's Theological Quarterly* 28 (1985) 287-94.

though the Church might be defined as the "body of Christ," this was taken as mere metaphor, implying no necessary connection with eucharistic participation in Christ's body and blood.[2]

While this approach to the eucharist by no means has disappeared, liturgical renewal together with rediscovery of the eucharistic ecclesiology of Christian antiquity has encouraged greater appreciation of the ecclesial significance of the eucharist, both within the churches and in ecumenical discussion. "The eucharist as a sacrament of the gospel is the fullest presentation of God's love in Jesus Christ by the power of the Holy Spirit."[3] In it "Christ makes effective among us the eternal benefits of his victory and elicits and renews our response of faith, thanksgiving and self-surrender."[4] It is "the sacrament of Christ himself. It becomes the foretaste of eternal life, the 'medicine of immortality,' the sign of the kingdom to come. The sacrament of the Christ event thus becomes identical with the sacrament of the holy eucharist ..."[5] The eucharist therefore can be described as "at once the source and climax of the church's life."[6] For the Church is "essentially 'the eucharistic community.'"[7] "When the church celebrates the eucharist it realizes 'what it is,' the body of Christ ... it becomes that which it is called to be by baptism and chrismation [confirmation]."[8] "The Eucharist actualizes the Church ... The Church celebrating the Eucharist becomes fully itself; that is *koinonia*, fellowship—communion."[9] The old disjunction between the *corpus Christi mysticum* and the *corpus Christi eucharisticum* is overcome: "The identity of the church as the body of Christ is both expressed and effectively proclaimed by its being centered in, and partaking of, his body and blood."[10] "The Church is the one indivisible Body of Christ in which the believers, as members of this Body, are united with Christ as its Head and with one another. The supreme expression and the perennial source of this unity is the sacrament of the Eucharist."[11]

This cento of quotations by no means exhausts the understanding of the eucharist presented in the various bilateral statements from which it is drawn, nor does it suggest the nuances that at points distinguish them one from another. Yet it does convey in summary fashion a basic conviction underlying both these statements and the WCC Faith and Order statement on *Baptism, Eucharist, Ministry*. The Church makes the eucharist: such was the tacit assumption behind older discussions of the subject. But ecumenical discussion today also affirms the converse: the eucharist makes the Church. A reciprocal relationship exists between them, so that "without the eucharistic community there is no full ecclesial community, and without the ecclesial community there is no real eucharistic community."[12] "Thus, on the one hand, the church celebrates the eucharist as the expression here and now of the heavenly liturgy; but on the other hand, the eucharist builds up the church in the sense that through it the Spirit of the risen Christ fashions the church into the body of Christ."[13]

Eucharist and Ministry

The eucharist makes the Church what it is called to be. It is both source and criterion of that impulse to renewal, unity and mission which characterizes the Church.[14] Further, "it is the eucharist which is the source of continuing scrutiny of the organization and life of the church,"[15] so that in the Church "the institutional elements should be nothing but a visible reflection of the reality of the mystery."[16] This line of thinking, when pursued, has important consequences for our understanding of ministry in the Church.

Virtually every bilateral and multilateral statement concerning ministry has begun by affirming that "the fundamental ministry is Christ's own ministry, whose goal is to reconcile all people to God and to each other and to bring them into a new community in which they can grow together to their full freedom as children of God."[17] The whole Church participates in this ministry of Christ, in his kingly priesthood; "each member contributes to that total ministry in a different fashion; there is a distribution of diverse gifts (cf. I Cor 12:4-11), and every baptized believer exercises his or her share in the total priesthood differently."[18] The bilaterals and multilaterals have also affirmed that a "special ministry" or "ordained ministry" has always existed within the Church and is essential for the Church, though terminology for it has varied.[19] But what is the relationship between this "special ministry" and that proper to the entire Church? Here the model of the Church as eucharistic assembly can provide helpful insights. In the eucharist the faithful come together in one body; their diverse gifts and forms of service are brought into unity and harmony because there is one who presides,[20] gathering the scattered grains of wheat into one eucharistic loaf,[21] recalling Christ's words at the

Last Supper, standing—like Christ—before God in the place of all the faithful, standing—again like Christ—before the faithful in the place of God.[22] Seen in this perspective, the "special ministry" does not replace or duplicate other ministries, much less provide a superior version of them. Rather, the special ministry of presiding is above all a ministry of unity, by which and in which the diverse aspects of Christ's ministry are manifested as one and whole.

The bilateral and multilateral statements generally single out three principal functions as essential and specific to the "special ministry": ministry of word, ministry of sacrament and—with these—ministry of *episcopê*, of oversight and pastoral care.[23] How are these functions to be integrated, so that ministry of the word will be organically joined to that of sacrament and not simply parallel to it;[24] so that *episcopê* will be organically joined to both and not simply an external administrative office? Here too the eucharistic model is helpful. If we recognize "the central act of the ordained ministry as presiding at the eucharist," this is because in it "the ministry of word, sacrament and pastoral care is perfected."[25] For the eucharist itself "is inseparably sacrament and word since in it the incarnate word sanctifies in the Spirit."[26] Sacrament "constitutes a proclamation of the word under the form of doxology and prayer" while "the word proclaimed is the word made flesh and became sacramental."[27] So also the various tasks implicit in *episcopê*—teaching, supervision, pastoral care, discernment as expressed in ordination and penitential discipline—are above all extensions and practical expressions of the word proclaimed in the eucharistic assembly.[28] In these tasks too the "special minister" is revealed not as an impersonal functionary or autocrat but as a "minister of Christ fashioning the unity of his body and so creating communion through his body."[29]

The "special ministry" has a twofold aspect: "The ordained minister is called and enabled by the Holy Spirit to be the representative person who focuses in his ministry the manifold ministries of the whole church. He is a sign of the gospel and of the oneness of Christ's church, both to the church and to the world; an ambassador of Christ who bids men to be reconciled to God and declares to them the forgiveness of sins; a priest who embodies the priesthood of all believers in which he shares, and by his ministry serves and sustains it."[30] In his liturgical action, he "has a twofold ministry: as an icon of Christ, acting in the name of Christ, towards the community; and also as a representative of the community expressing the priesthood of the faithful."[31] This excludes first of all any notion that "those consecrated to the special ministry are given a *potestas* and derive a dignity from Christ without reference to the believing community."[32] Rather, "the ordained minister manifests and exercises the authority of Christ in the way Christ himself revealed God's authority to the world: in and through *communion*."[33] His function "is closely bound to the eucharistic assembly over which he presides."[34] He cannot be separated from the Church any more than the Church can be separated from him. For this reason, "ordination, or setting apart for the exercise of these special services takes place within the context of the believing community."[35] "Because ministry is in and for the community and because ordination is an act in which the whole Church of God is involved, the prayer and laying on of hands takes place within the context of the eucharist."[36] At the same time, "the office of ministry stands over against the community as well as within it."[37] That is, when the ordained minister proclaims the gospel in word and sacrament or expresses it in the various acts of *episcopê*, he does so with the authority of Christ, and not merely on the basis of his personal convictions or as delegated representative of the community. This too is expressed in ordination, in which both prayers and gestures (laying on of hands) and context (the eucharist) emphasize the divine initiative in calling and setting apart; "it is not the community which produces and authorizes the office but the living Christ who bestows it on the community and incorporates this office into its life."[38]

A Tool and a Challenge

The bilateral statements cited here, like the Faith and Order Commission's *Baptism, Eucharist, Ministry*, would stress that "an understanding of the ministry must ... start from the nature of the Church."[39] Most of them, even more emphatically than *Baptism, Eucharist, Ministry*, would in turn stress that the Church is not just community, but *eucharistic* community, that it is above all when gathered in eucharistic fellowship that the Church realizes itself as locus for the communion of men and women with each other and with the Father through the Son in the Spirit.

Implications of this understanding of the Church for the understanding of the ministry have not been fully explored in the bilaterals. But in one area at least, that of validity of ministry, a veritable revolution has been taking place. Mutual recognition of ministries is increasingly becoming a matter of mutual recognition of eucharistic communities as ecclesial entities, reversing the narrowly juridical approach to "valid orders" that has prevailed since the Middle Ages.[40]

Further exploration of the eucharistic model of the Church might help to advance discussion of other ecumenically sensitive subjects as well—pneumatology, for example. To be sure, the model has certain limitations and weaknesses. There is always the danger of anachronism, of making an idealized early church order normative in every detail for all ages and places. Yet its central intuition should be recognized: the Church's structures, including its ministry, must be fully transparent to its nature and ultimate goal as revealed in the eucharist. Thus understood, the eucharistic model is not just a tool for advancing ecumenical discussion. It also challenges us to reexamine the spiritual vitality of our own church structures.

In the early Church the work of reconciliation and recreation accomplished by Christ in the Holy Spirit was effectively proclaimed and realized not just *within* the structures of the eucharistic assembly but also *by* them. The means of proclamation and realization were one with their essential content. The early Christians did not go to church; they "gathered as church" (cf. 1 Cor 11:18). They did not "receive communion"; they entered into it, with God and with each other. In the midst of this broken and fragmented world, they became, by the power of the Holy Spirit, one body in Christ, in whom "there is neither Jew nor Greek, slave nor free, male nor female." In very tangible ways they experienced and at the same time expressed the Church's catholicity, that all-embracing quality which makes it impossible to identify the Church with a particular class, nationality, special interest group, locality or community. Do our church structures today encourage or even permit us and those around us to experience so vividly this essential *nota ecclesiae?* Even if our present structures were adequate to the third century, are they adequate to the twentieth? Do they effectively proclaim Christ's victory over the divisions of this fallen world, or do they in fact serve to perpetuate and even exacerbate them? The eucharistic model of the Church, if rightly understood, does not allow us to be content simply with preserving the structures of antiquity (a constant temptation for the Orthodox) or with replicating them (cf. the new appreciation of the episcopate in Protestant circles). On the contrary, it challenges us to reexamine the Church's structures, past and present, in the light of the Church's unchanging nature and purpose: to realize in the midst of the earth God's work of salvation. Let us not decline this challenge in favor of the charms of an ecclesiastical Williamsburg.

NOTES

1 Thus *In Quest of a Church of Christ Uniting* (Consultation on Church Union, Princeton NJ 1980) 30ff.

2 Ibid. 19-23.

3 International Methodist-Roman Catholic Joint Commission, "Dublin Report" (1976) ¶ 52a; in *Growth in Agreement: Reports and Agreed Statements of Interconfessional Religious Conversations on a World Level*, ed H. Meyer and L. Vischer (Paulist Press, Paramus, NJ 1984) 280.

4 Anglican-Roman Catholic International Commission, "Windsor Statement" (1971) ¶ 3; *Growth in Agreement* 67.

5 Orthodox-Roman Catholic Joint International Commission, "The Church, the Eucharist and the Trinity" (Munich 1982) I.2; in *Origins* 12 (August 13, 1982) 157.

6 Joint Roman Catholic-Lutheran Commission, "The Eucharist" (1978) ¶ 26; *Growth in Agreement* 188.

7 Reformed-Roman Catholic Dialogue, "The Presence of Christ in Church and World" (1977) ¶ 88; *Growth in Agreement* 352.

8 Orthodox-Roman Catholic ... I. 4b; *Origins* 158.

9 Commission for Anglican-Orthodox Joint Doctrinal Discussion, "Moscow Statement" (1976) ¶ 24; *Growth in Agreement* 45.

10 Anglican-Roman Catholic ... ¶ 3; *Growth in Agreement* 67.

11 Joint Orthodox-Old Catholic Theological Commission, "Ecclesiology" (1977, 1979) III.2.1; *Growth in Agreement* 310.

12 Roman Catholic-Lutheran ... ¶ 26; *Growth in Agreement* 188.

13 Orthodox-Roman Catholic ... I.4c; *Origins* 158.

14 Reformed-Roman Catholic ... ¶ 88; *Growth in Agreement* 353. Cf. Anglican-Roman Catholic ... ¶ 3; *Growth in Agreement* 67.

15 Reformed-Roman Catholic ... ¶ 90; *Growth in Agreement* 353.

16 Orthodox-Roman Catholic ... II.1; *Origins* 159.

17 Methodist-Roman Catholic ... ¶ 77 *Growth in Agreement* 285.

18 Reformed-Roman Catholic ... ¶ 96; *Growth in Agreement* 355.

19 Anglican-Roman Catholic International Commission, "Canterbury Statement" especially ¶ 5-7; *Growth in Agreement* 74-75. Anglican-Lutheran Conversation, "Pulach Report" (1972) ¶ 76; *Growth in Agreement* 24. Lutheran-Roman Catholic ... "Malta Report" (1972) especially ¶ 56; *Growth in Agreement* 171. Methodist-Roman Catholic ... ¶ 82; *Growth in Agreement* 285. Reformed-Roman Catholic ... ¶ 97-9; *Growth in Agreement* 355-56. Commission on Faith and Order, "The Ordained Ministry" ¶ 13ff; *Growth in Agreement* 381.

20 Cf. Justin Martyr, *First Apology* 67.

21 Cf. *Didachê* 9.

22 Cf. Ignatius, *Magn.* 6: "Let the bishop preside in the place of God ..."

23 Anglican-Roman Catholic ... "Canterbury Statement" ¶ 9-11; *Growth in Agreement* 75-6. Anglican-Lutheran ... ¶ 77-9; *Growth in Agreement* 24. Lutheran-Roman Catholic ... ¶ 89; *Growth in Agreement* 286. Reformed-Roman Catholic ... ¶ 97; *Growth in Agreement* 355. Faith and Order ¶ 15 *et passim; Growth in Agreement* 381 ff.

24 Cf. the comments of J. Zizioulas in *The Orthodox Church and the Churches of the Reformation: A Survey of Orthodox-Protestant Dialogues* (World Council of Churches, Geneva 1975) 57.

25 Methodist-Roman Catholic ... ¶ 97; *Growth in Agreement* 287.

26 Orthodox-Roman Catholic ... II.2; *Origins* 159.

27 Ibid.

28 Ibid. II.3.

29 Ibid.

30 Methodist-Roman Catholic ... ¶ 98; *Growth in Agreement* 288.

31 Anglican-Orthodox ... ¶ 27; *Growth in Agreement* 45.

32 Reformed-Roman Catholic ... ¶ 97; *Growth in Agreement* 355.

33 Faith and Order ¶ 18; *Growth in Agreement* 382.

34 Orthodox-Roman Catholic ... II.3; *Origins* 159.

35 Reformed-Roman Catholic... ¶ 97; *Growth in Agreement* 355.

36 Anglican-Roman Catholic... "Canterbury Statement" ¶ 14; *Growth in Agreement* 77.

37 Lutheran-Roman Catholic ... ¶ 50; *Growth in Agreement* 170.

38 Reformed-Roman Catholic ... ¶ 98; *Growth in Agreement* 356.

39 Faith and Order ¶ 2; *Growth in Agreement* 379.

40 Cf. Zizioulas (n 24 *supra*) 57.

Chapter 6

Collegiality and Primacy in Orthodox Ecclesiology*

In the Creed we confess our belief in "one holy, catholic and apostolic Church," just as we confess "one God, the Father almighty," "one Lord Jesus Christ," and "the Holy Spirit, the Lord, the Giver of life." The Church is an object of belief, a part of our faith. Yet there exists—for the Orthodox at least—no dogma of the Church analogous to the trinitarian dogma of Nicea and I Constantinople, or the christological dogma of Ephesus, Chalcedon and the subsequent ecumenical councils. Even a fully developed doctrine—like that concerning the procession of the Holy Spirit—is lacking. The Church is described, or rather she is magnified: new paradise, the spiritual Eden, the sanctuary of God, an earthly heaven.[1] But she is not defined. Even in the Roman Catholic Church—precocious in the writing of treatises *de ecclesia*—the elaboration of dogmatic definitions is comparatively recent, and the initial stage of this elaboration, Vatican I's *Pastor Aeternus,* could prompt Newman's complaint: "When has definition of doctrine *de fide* been a luxury of devotion and not a stern painful necessity?"[2]

This situation certainly has changed over the last century, for Orthodox and non-Orthodox alike. Ecclesiology has become a major element in the theological enterprise, and central to virtually every discussion of ecclesiology is the theme of this Congress: the relationship between local autonomy and central power in the Church. In part this is due to internal needs of the churches. For example, post-Vatican II Roman Catholic theologians have had the delicate task of harmonizing *Lumen Gentium's* state-

* Originally presented under the title "Common Comprehension of Christians Concerning Autonomy and Central Power in the Church in View of Orthodox Theology" at the Fourth Congress of the Gesellschaft für das Recht der Ostkirchen, Regensburg 1978, and printed in *Kanon* 4 (1979) 100-12.

ments on collegiality with *Pastor Aeternus'* declaration that the Roman Pontiff is endowed with a "power of jurisdiction over the universal Church" that is "full and supreme ... ordinary and immediate" (ch. 3), and that his *ex cathedra* statements are "infallible and irreformable *ex sese, non autem ex consensu Ecclesiae*" (ch. 4).[3] So also, internal needs have compelled the Orthodox to examine the meaning of primacy in the Church, and more concretely, the role of the patriarchate of Constantinople. In the nineteenth century, Orthodox responses to Vatican I could argue that the system of autocephalous churches—utterly independent yet united in faith—was an alternative to papalism. The weaknesses of this argument have become increasingly apparent. Like the pre-World War I system of sovereign nation states, on which in many respects it was modeled, the system of autocephalous churches has failed to meet the demands made on it in our tragic century. Yet there is no consensus on alternatives. While the patriarch of Constantinople is acknowledged by all as "first among equals," what this priority involves in the actual life of the Orthodox churches in our day is by no means clear. The line between legitimate primacy and "neo-papalism" has not been drawn. The result has been a series of confrontations. What is the status of the Church of Poland, the Church of Czechoslovakia, the "Paris exarchate," the Orthodox Church in America? What is the status of the so-called diaspora in general? And who is to determine these matters? With good reason the latest commission charged with preparing a Great and Holy Council of the Orthodox churches has placed the problems of autocephaly, the diaspora and the diptychs (i.e., the ranking of the churches) high on the agenda.

Yet these various internal needs cannot alone account for the present preoccupation with ecclesiology. Ecclesiology has become an ecumenical enterprise. Certainly Orthodox theology—and indeed the very existence of the ancient, but distinctly non-Roman churches of the East—has influenced modern Roman Catholic thinking on ecclesiological questions. And at the same time, Vatican II has stimulated not only Roman Catholic, but also Protestant and Orthodox thought. Certainly for the Orthodox, discussion of the place in the Church of Constantinople, New Rome, inevitably raises the subject of Old Rome and of its role not only in the Church's first millennium but also in the future.

The main lines of the modern Orthodox contribution to ecclesiology are well known and need only to be sketched here:

(1) The point of departure is the Ignatian vision of the local church: the faithful coming together as Church, *epi tô autô,* (1 Cor 11:17, 20; 14:23, 26), becoming the body of Christ in the eucharist, becoming one out of many ("As this piece of bread was scattered over the hills and then was brought together and made one ..." *Didachê* 9); with the bishop personifying this unity, summing up the local church in himself ("I received your large congregation in the person of Onesimus, your bishop in this world ..." Ignatius, *Eph.* 1), standing—like Christ—before God in the place of all the faithful, standing—again like Christ—before the faithful in the place of God ("Let the bishop preside in the place of God..." Ignatius, *Magn.* 6).

(2) This eucharistic assembly under the presidency of the bishop is the Church in all its fulness, not just a part of the Church. The body of Christ, the temple of the Holy Spirit, possessing all the *notae ecclesiae,* it is the basic unit on which all subsequent speculation must be based, the primary experience underlying all effort at definition. But the Church that dwells in Corinth has the same unity, the same fulness as the Church that dwells in Jerusalem, Antioch, Rome ...

(3) This essential unity of the local churches means the essential unity and equality of their bishops. Hence episcopal consecration, with its plurality of consecrators: "It is not the transfer of a gift by those who possess it, but the manifestation of the fact that the same gift, which they have received in the Church from God, has now been given to this bishop in this Church."[5] Hence the council of bishops, with its emphasis on unanimity, with each bishop subscribing, giving his own testimony to the truth held by all: here we have an expression of the common mind of the episcopate, an expression of the authority *of* all, not a supreme power *over* all.[6]

(4) But this equality of local churches and of bishops does not mean uniformity, just as unity of essence does not exclude plurality of utterly unique hypostases. Each local church is unique; and of these, some may "preside in love" (Ignatius, *Rom.* prol.), some may more completely and perfectly express the common faith because they do not try to possess it for themselves alone but share all that they are with the others. Many factors may contribute to the potential for presidency: antiquity and

apostolicity of foundation, the glory of martyrdom and suffering for Christ, geopolitical advantages, size, wealth. But the presidency itself consists not in *having* any or all of these elements but in *sharing* them, in making the patrimony of one church—of the first church—the patrimony of all. A favorite comparison at this point: God the Father, who shares all that He is with the Son, the precise image of the person of the Father, coequal and consubstantial with Him.[7] A favorite proof-text: Apostolic Canon 34, with its careful balance of conciliarity and primacy and its striking trinitarian doxology:

> The bishops of every nation must acknowledge him who is first among them and account him as their head, and do nothing of consequence without his consent; but each may do those things which concern his own parish, and the country places which belong to it. But neither let him who is the first do anything without the consent of all. For so there will be oneness of mind, and God will be glorified through the Lord in the Holy Spirit.[8]

This ecclesiology, at least in its broad outlines, today is generally accepted among the Orthodox. Once identified chiefly with the late Fr Afanasieff and émigré Russian theologians, "eucharistic ecclesiology" has been given both balance and scholarly precision quite independently by Prof. (now Metropolitan) John Zizioulas, a Greek.[9] It is also worth noting that its fundamental presuppositions underlie Metropolitan Maximus of Sardes' remarkable recent study of *The Oecumenical Patriarchate in the Orthodox Church.*[10] Yet this approach to ecclesiology is not limited to the Orthodox. A very similar approach may be found among Protestants (witness Werner Elert's remarkable study of *Eucharist and Church Fellowship in the First Four Centuries*[11]) and also Roman Catholics: Hertling, Congar, Lecuyer, Le Guillou, Hamer, Ratzinger ...[12] Contrasted with the heavily juridical "universal ecclesiology" that has developed from the Middle Ages is the "*communio* ecclesiology" of the early Church, with its emphasis on the local eucharistic community: the Church of God, the effective presence of the whole Christ in a given place, and not just the branch office of a universal organization; with its emphasis as well on the communion existing between these local churches, as expressed both by episcopal collegiality and by reference to the central church of this *communio*, the Church of Rome.

After centuries of divergence it seems that Christians are now moving towards convergence, towards an ecumenical ecclesiology. The Lutheran/

Roman Catholic dialogue in the United States has produced an important common statement on the papal primacy;[13] Anglicans and Roman Catholics meeting in Venice in 1976 elaborated a major declaration on authority in the church;[14] a recent American book can raise the question of *A Pope for All Christians?*[15] Today ecclesiology is not only the focus of ecumenical activity. It is also an area which conjures up the prospect of ecumenical agreement, of common definition arising neither from "luxury of devotion" nor from the "stern painful necessity" of excluding heretics.

Yet here a note of caution must be sounded. Certainly great strides have been made toward a "common comprehension of Christians" on ecclesiological matters. We use the same words; we refer to the same sources. Yet do we understand these words, do we approach these sources, in the same way? Or do differences of emphasis, often hidden but inevitably present after centuries of estrangement, still make our ecclesiologies not only different, but fundamentally incompatible, despite their considerable concordance on a verbal level? It is to the task of locating and exploring some of these differences that I should like to turn in this paper.

A first area that must be explored is our very understanding of "communion"—certainly one of the key words in current ecumenical discussion. Both Roman Catholics and Orthodox speak of the deleterious effects of "universal ecclesiology" and of the need for an "ecclesiology of communion." Yet a difference in emphasis can be noted. Typical of the Roman Catholic approach, I would say, is Hertling's classic study of *communio.* "*Communio* is the bond that united the bishops and the faithful, the bishops among themselves, and the faithful among themselves..." It is "the union of believers, the community of the faithful, and therefore the Church itself."[16] Stress is on the horizontal fellowship that exists between Christians and between their churches, and also on the ways of maintaining this fellowship: the diptychs, exchange of letters, reference to preeminent churches in the communion ... Though Hertling tries not to enter into controversy over the original meaning of the phrase *communio sanctorum* in the "Apostles' Creed," he clearly is inclined to see *sanctorum* as the genitive of *sancti* (masc.) rather than of *sancta* (neut.), making the phrase refer to fellowship with the saints rather than to partaking of the Holy Things, i.e., the eucharist.[17]

Quite different is the Orthodox approach. When theologians like Olivier Clement write on "Orthodox Ecclesiology as an Ecclesiology of Communion,"[18] it is to stress that communion—*koinônia*—is first of all communion with the Father through participation—*metalêpsis*—in Him who alone is holy, Jesus Christ, whom the Spirit makes present for us in the sacrament of the eucharist.[19] While by no means denying the horizontal aspect of communion, Orthodox theology would emphasize the priority of the vertical: the Church as community and fellowship must have as its basis communion with God, as realized above all in the eucharist.

But to speak of the vertical is at once to speak of the eschatological. The eucharist is the banquet of God's kingdom. Through it we commune here and now in realities yet to come. It is not simply a remembrance of Him who walked on earth with us and was crucified and rose again for our sakes. In the *anamnêsis* of the Liturgy of St John Chrysostom we remember the future as well: "Remembering the cross, the tomb, the resurrection on the third day, the ascension into heaven, the sitting at the right hand, *and the second and glorious coming ...*" Christ—of whom we partake sacramentally in the eucharist, whose body we become—is not just a figure from the past. He is also the "last Adam"—*eschatos Adam* (1 Cor 15:45)—the eschatological man.

The eschatological thrust of the Orthodox understanding of communion has important corollaries for ecclesiology, and above all for the understanding of apostolicity, as Zizioulas has shown.[20] Zizioulas has distinguished two principal images used in Biblical and early Christian literature to describe the nature and role of the apostles. In the first, spatial and historical, they are seen as individuals sent out by Christ's command into all the world to preach the Gospel and to found churches. But in the other, the eschatological, they are gathered in one place as an indivisible college around the one Lord: "when the Son of Man shall sit on His glorious throne, you who have followed me will also sit on twelve thrones, judging the twelve tribes of Israel" (Mt 19:28). Historically, one church may be established by Peter, another by Paul, another by a missionary hundreds of years later. Yet all are equally and fully apostolic, just as they are one, holy and catholic. For the structure of each local church—the bishop surrounded by the college of presbyters, the deacons and all the faithful—has a direct iconic relationship to the kingdom where Christ stands surrounded by the apostles.

This eschatological image, so striking especially in Ignatius, shifts with Cyprian to that of the apostolic college surrounding St Peter. For Ignatius, the bishop had held "the place of God" or was the image of Christ.[21] For Cyprian, the bishop occupies the *cathedra Petri*. Yet even in this altered image, the eschatological is not completely subsumed in the historical and spatial. For *each* bishop occupies the *cathedra Petri*;[22] the *protos* is not separated from the rest of the apostolic college; the keys which he wields are the keys of the kingdom.

In Byzantium such images continue to shift, often with bewildering abruptness. A wide variety of sources must be considered: works of exegesis, hagiography and the like as well as controversial literature, whether appealing to Rome or polemicizing against her. Consequently, any attempt to pick out a single and altogether consistent line of thought must be held suspect. A few general observations may be made, however. First, there is little interest in what we have termed the "historical" argument for apostolicity, apart from some clumsy efforts to oppose the apostolicity of Constantinople—supposedly founded by St Andrew, the "first-called" and the elder brother of Peter—to that of Rome.[23] For the most part Byzantine writers reject emphatically any suggestion that apostolic authority—or Petrine or "Andrean" authority—is limited or uniquely linked to a particular see. "The Italians have made the universal teacher (i.e., Peter) the bishop of one city," complains Mesarites.[24] Or as another popular argument goes: the Church is not of Paul or of Apollo or of Cephas but of Christ, its one foundation, and is established on one rock, the confession of Peter.[25] Constantinople could—and did—call herself apostolic without any reference to the Andrew legend;[26] a late Byzantine writer could speak of the Pope as "the successor of Peter *and of all the apostles*";[27] Byzantine ecclesiastical literature could see the image of Peter in every faithful bishop:[28] all this was possible because in the East apostolicity—and for that matter "Petrinity"—was not just a product of history. A later Byzantine polemicist expresses the Eastern position with almost painful precision: "Every orthodox bishop is the vicar of Christ and the successor of the apostles, so that, if all the bishops of the world detach themselves from the true faith and there remains but one guardian of the true dogmas ... it is in him that the faith of the divine Peter will be preserved."[29] And: "Bishops established by Peter are successors not only of Peter, but also of the other apostles; just as the bishops established by other apostles are successors of Peter."[30] The eschatological perspective still prevails: in each local church the bishop "stands in the place of God"; in each local church the apostolic college gathered around Peter is reflected.

Given this radical equality of bishops—and of the local churches to which they are so intimately linked—whence arises primacy? Byzantine writers are quite explicit on this point: "It is not according to a plan or arrangement of a spiritual nature that the thrones of our churches have acquired superiority or inferiority, but according to the order of preeminence and subordination of the principalities of the world ... Preeminence is not accorded to the churches on account of the burial places of the apostles, but on account of the disposition of the holy and ecumenical councils."[31] Primacy arises not from "apostolicity" understood in the strictly historical sense, as Rome would claim, but from that "principle of accommodation" of church organization to the structures of civil government which the late Fr Dvornik has so ably described.[32]

The strengths and weaknesses of this "principle" are manifest. At its best, accommodation can be the Church's "dynamic and living ability *to preserve* her own norms, her own principles of polity, her own divinely established eucharistic structures in the midst of contemporary realities."[33] But what is to prevent accommodation from becoming subordination? What is to prevent a complete identification of the interests of the Church with those of the civil authority? If this fate was averted in Byzantium it was precisely because the Byzantines, however avidly they might have sought privileges and honors, prerogatives and primacies, never identified these with the *esse* of the Church, which is revealed in the eschatological perspective of her sacramental life. The thrones of this world are not the thrones of the kingdom.

But if primacy and other forms of church organization above the level of the local church do not belong to the *esse* of the Church, they certainly do belong to her *bene esse*, to use the favorite expression of many these days. Primacy exists "for the good order—*eutaksia*—of the Church."[34] The need for *eutaksia*, or simply for *taksis* (for Byzantines always viewed order as a great good): this, and not an abstract principle of conformity to civil structure, is the reason for the preeminence or subordination of sees. Interesting in this regard are Byzantine discussions of the "pentarchy." The subject, so far removed from reality, gave perfect opportunity for speculation on the ideal: an ideal of harmony, coordination, mutual support, in which "he that holds the first place does not boast or lord it over the second, or the second over the third."[35]

And while order is the principal theme of the Byzantine canonists, that of service is not altogether absent. Our canonical texts speak far more often of *presbeia* and *timê* than they do of *diakonia* or *leitourgia.* Yet it was not completely forgotten that precedence and honor in the Church exist only in view of ministry and service. Certainly the service especially of St John Chrysostom gave substance to talk of Constantinople's *presbeia timês* and paved the way for the specific *rights* which Chalcedon later gave to that see. While most Byzantine polemicists dated Rome's primacy in the Church only to the time of Constantine, at least one conceded that it was of pre-Constantinian origin and had been established in order to give the bishop of Rome greater authority in defending the interests of the Church before the pagan authorities.[36]

At this point it is important to note not only how and why primacy arises, but also how it is expressed—and how it is *not* expressed. The West since the thirteenth century has distinguished between the "power of orders" and the "power of jurisdiction," sometimes to the point of separation, and has understood primacy above all in terms of jurisdiction.[37] The East, however, never developed a notion of jurisdiction apart from orders. The very term *dikaiodôsio* is a modern one, an effort to translate the Latin *jurisdictio*, and has no resonance in the eastern canonical tradition. On the one hand, ordination for the East is never "absolute," but rather is always tied to pastoral ministry in a specific local church.[38] On the other hand, any form of pastoral ministry is viewed as inconceivable without a sacramental expression of this in the context of the church community, for it is a charism—a gift—bestowed in and for the community. A primacy of supra-episcopal jurisdictional power would necessarily presuppose the existence of a distinct and new sacramental order. So at least argues Nilus Cabasilas:

> When the Pope is ordained by bishops he does not receive a higher power than bishop: no one can give what he does not have. Therefore he is not superior to

bishops; he is as one of them, and subject to all the laws to which the episcopal order is subject ... Whence he cannot regulate ecclesiastical matters without their counsel, as canon 34 of the apostles indicates.[39]

For the eastern canonical tradition—at least in its earliest expressions—a primate, whether regional or universal, does not possess superior "jurisdiction" which could be superimposed upon that of his brother bishops. As a bishop, he enjoys full authority of pastoral ministry in his own church; there he "stands in the place of God." But his supra-diocesan function is not of the same nature as this diocesan authority. He does not "stand in the place of God" in another's diocese unless by invitation. He is by no means a universal bishop with "power of jurisdiction over the universal Church" that is "full and supreme ... ordinary and immediate."

As Cabasilas's reference to Apostolic Canon 34 suggests, the primate's supra-diocesan role is placed a collegial context: the bishops of the province may "do nothing of consequence without his consent ... but neither let him who is the first do anything without the consent of all." He does not, properly speaking, have power over his suffragans since he cannot choose or consecrate them by himself nor judge or transfer them from one see to another without synodal action. But his primacy is not simply one of honor: a high title, chairmanship of meetings and the first seat at banquets. Something more is involved in primacy, and that something, I suggest, may be found in the concept of *phrontis, sollicitudo.*

According to canon 9 of the Council of Antioch, for the most part a reiteration of the provisions of Apostolic Canon 34: "It behooves the bishops in every province to acknowledge the bishop who presides in the metropolis, and who is charged with concern for the whole province —*tên phrontida anadekhesthai pasês tês eparkhias*—because all men of business come together from every quarter to the metropolis." Concern, care, supervision, solicitude: this is exercised on the provincial level in a number of concrete ways, but chiefly in the supervision of episcopal elections (Antioch canon 19) and in the reception of appeals (Sardica canon 14). The metropolitan's *phrontis* is to see that the canons are observed, that due process is maintained. But this *phrontis* is not limited to the provincial level. "All men of business come together to the metropolis—*en tê metropolei syntrekhein ...*" One's thought turns to St Ireneus' words about Rome: "*ad* hanc enim ecclesiam propter potentiorem principalitatem necesse est omnem *convenire* ecclesiam ..." Is it not likely that the lost Greek original for *convenire ad* was *syntrekhein en*, as in the canon of Antioch? In any case, just as everyone has recourse to the metropolis on a provincial level, so on the universal level, all roads lead to Rome, whose "presidency in love" in the early Church consisted precisely in her solicitude. It is interesting to note that Batiffol, after examining virtually all early Christian evidence on the role of Rome in the Church, concludes: "The papacy of the first centuries is the authority exercised by the Church of Rome among other churches which consists in *caring after* their conformity with the authentic tradition of faith ..."[40]

The solicitude—the "all-embracing pastoral concern"[41]—of the first see knows no limits of time and place, but it does have juridical limits. It possesses moral authority, but it is not a "central power" in the Church. Its only power—but that a great one—is the power of love, which does not demand, but rather elicits acceptance. "Acceptance," or "reception": the importance of this concept for the Orthodox is well-known.[42] If the ways in which solicitude is exercised are to have the force of law, they must be "received" or "accepted" as having that force. An example can be seen in the Sardican appeal canons. They were not "received" in Africa at the time of the affair of Apiarius, and hence their provisions for transmarine appeal were rejected. However, they were "received" in the East via the *Synagogê in Fifty Titles* and the *Syntagma in Fourteen Titles* in the mid-sixth century. Therefore at the time of the Council of Constantinople in 861, appeal to Rome was accepted as a distinct possibility, but only within the terms of the canons. These provided that, if appeal is made, the Pope may review the evidence and order a new trial, and if need be yet another trial, this time with the participation of presbyters sent by Rome *a latere*. If appeal is made: that was the difficulty in 861, for Ignatius—supposedly on whose behalf the Roman legates had come—categorically declared: "Ego non appellavi Romam, nec appello"—"I did not appeal nor do I appeal to Rome."[43] When expressions of solicitude go beyond the canons accepted by all, they may be accepted, but they also may be rejected, as was the case, for example, with Rome's decision in favor of Emperor Leo VI's fourth marriage.[44]

By this period, however, Rome had quite a different understanding of "acceptance." Fr Congar describes this very well:

For Rome, the papal decisions ... had the force of law in the universal church *ex sese*, it may be said. Of course, Rome spoke of "acceptance," but she did not understand it in the sense that this acceptance gave the decisions their force. Acceptance is but obedience to decisions having their force in themselves, by reason of the authority which promulgated them.[45]

The language of *sollicitudo* has given way to that of *plenitudo potestatis*. The "ocular" imagery which characterized the former: oversight, supervision, review ... has given way to imagery drawn from law and government, to words like "rule," "power" and "dominion."

In the East, too, there are changes in the course of the Middle Ages. Ties of bishop to his local church, of metropolitan to his province, erode as transfers become common and election and ordination are removed from the context of the local church. From an *ad hoc* gathering, the *synodos endêmousa* becomes a permanent organ of government, making the bishops *separated* from their churches a collective "central power" over those actually involved in the pastoral ministry. In short, we find the necessary preconditions for a "universal ecclesiology." Yet the expression that this new ecclesiology takes in the East is quite different from that in the West. In the West, the Church comes to be seen above all as a body politic, as a society; its hierarchy has the obligation to sanctify, to teach, but above all to rule.[46] In the East the characteristic note is caught by Nicetas Stethatus in his treatise *On the Hierarchy*.[47] Distressed that Pseudo-Dionysius had not fully worked out parallels between the celestial and the ecclesiastical hierarchies, Stethatus adds—in an extremely wooden fashion—patriarchs, metropolitans and archbishops to the orders of those who are divinely chosen as illuminators and sanctifiers. The Church spread over all the earth is united in a liturgy which reflects that of the heavenly choirs.

This difference in emphasis can be seen in many aspects of church life. The political image of the Church favored in the West readily lends itself to expression in concrete forms. For example, in the *Dictatus Papae* of Gregory VII we read that "The Pope alone may use the imperial insignia" (c. 8), "That he may depose emperors" (c. 12), "That for him alone it is lawful to enact new laws according to the needs of the time ..." (c. 7). The Pope is seen as supreme monarch, and as such he also is supreme legislator. In the East, on the other hand, the patriarch of Constantinople has never—to the best of my knowledge—been called *nomothetês*, though the emperor may be. His task is not "to enact laws" but, in the words of the *Epanagogê*, to "interpret the canons passed by the men of old and the decrees enacted by the holy councils" (c. 5) and to "handle and decide matters on the basis of what has been done and arranged ... by the early fathers in the ecumenical and provincial councils" (c. 6).

Examples of this sort could be multiplied showing that juridically the role of the patriarch—or any other "central power"—is a very limited one. Even within the "universal ecclesiology" which developed in Byzantium in the course of the Middle Ages, the patriarch's primacy is expressed above all in terms of ... solicitude. Particularly interesting in this regard are the patriarchal *acta* of the later Middle Ages, a period in which many have detected a Byzantine "neo-papalism."[48] Here is what Patriarch Philotheus Coccinus writes in 1370 to the Russian princes who had seceded from their metropolitan, Alexis, who at the time was regent of the Muscovite state:

> Since God has appointed Our Humility as leader of all Christians found anywhere in the *oikoumenê*, as protector and guardian [*kêdemona kai phrontistên*] of their souls, all of them depend on me, the father and teacher of them all. If that were possible, therefore, it would have been my duty to walk through the cities and countries everywhere on earth and teach in them the Word of God, doing so unfailingly, since such is our duty. But since it is beyond the capacity of one weak and helpless man to walk around the entire *oikoumenê*, Our Humility chooses the best among men, the most eminent in virtue, establishes and ordains them as pastors, teachers and high-priests, and sends them to the ends of the universe. One of them goes to your great country, to the multitudes which inhabit it, another reaches other areas of the earth, and still another goes elsewhere, so that each, in the country and place appointed him, enjoys territorial rights, and episcopal see, and all the rights of Our Humility.[49]

If read in the context of western church history, this text would indeed suggest papalism. Read in the context of Byzantine history, it can in part be dismissed as an example of Byzantine rhetoric. But note also the choice of words: "protector and guardian," "father and teacher." This is quite different from the language of Innocent III and Boniface VIII, or even of Leo I and Gelasius I. Phrases like *kêdemonia pantôn* might suggest a less-than-felicitous ecclesiology, but they should not be identified with *plenitudo potestatis*.

This brief historical survey suggests a paradox. In the course of late antiquity and the Middle Ages, the Roman Catholic Church insisted that its primacy was due not to contingencies of politics and history but to Christ's promise to Peter. Yet the vocabulary used to describe this primacy comes more and more to be that of the principalities of this world. The Byzantine Church, on the other hand, freely acknowledged that primacies depend on the order of the principalities of this world. Yet the vocabulary used for the most part sounds eminently evangelical. Once stated, this paradox may be discarded as a caricature, an oversimplification. Yet our histories have been different. Our vocabularies have been different. Certainly we need not be prisoners of history or of its words, as developments particularly within the Roman Catholic Church over the last several decades have shown. Yet as we come to use the same words, will we mean the same thing? Will there in fact be "oneness of mind," so that "God will be glorified through the Lord in the Holy Spirit?" Much depends on how well we learn to listen both to each other and to what our histories have to say to us today.

NOTES

1 Cf. the texts presented by Y. Congar, "Ecclesiological Awareness in the East and in the West from the Sixth to the Eleventh Century," in *The Unity of the Churches of God*, ed P. Sherwood (Baltimore 1963) 127-84.

2 Letter of January 28, 1870, quoted in W. Ward, *The Life of John Henry Cardinal Newman*, vol 2 (London 1912) 287-9.

3 Some would even speak of the need for "revision" of Vatican I: G. Thils, *La primauté pontificale: La doctrine de Vatican I, les voies d'une revision* (Gembloux 1972) and "The Theology of the Primacy: Towards a Revision," in *One in Christ* 10 (1974) 13-30.

4 P. Evdokimov, "Les principaux courants de l'écclésiologie orthodoxe au XIXe siècle," *Revue des sciences religieuses* 34 (1960) 70-2.

5 A. Schmemann, "The Idea of Primacy in Orthodox Ecclesiology," in *The Primacy of Peter* (London 1963) 41. Cf. Bp Pierre (L'Huillier), "La pluralité des consécrateurs dans les chirotonies épiscopales," *Messager de l'Exarchat du Patriarchat Russe en Europe Occidentale* 42-43 (1963) 102 ff.

6 On this point see J. Zizioulas, "The Development of Conciliar Structures to the Time of the First Ecumenical Council," in *Councils and the Ecumenical Movement*, World Council of Churches Studies 5 (Geneva 1968) 34-51.

7 Thus O. Clement, "Orthodox Ecclesiology as an Ecclesiology of Communion," *One in Christ* 6 (1970) 114-5.

8 Trans *The Seven Ecumenical Councils*, A Select Library of Nicene and Post-

Nicene Fathers, 2nd ser, vol 14, 596. Cf. P. Duprey, "The Synodal Structure of the Church in Eastern Theology," *One in Christ* 7 (1971) 153-5.

9 Of Afanasieff's major works only one has been translated from the Russian: *L'Eglise du Saint-Esprit* (Paris 1975); the main lines of his thought can be discerned in his essay "The Church Which Presides in Love," in *The Primacy of Peter* (London 1963) 57-110. The title of Zizioulas's major book, *The Unity of the Church in the Eucharist and the Bishop during the First Three Centuries* (in Greek, Athens 1965) suggests the main lines followed in recent versions of this approach to ecclesiology. His most recent work, *Being as Communion* (St Vladimir's Seminary Press, Crestwood, NY 1985) offers further development and refinement.

10 (Thessaloniki 1976).

11 (Saint Louis, MO 1966).

12 L. Hertling, *Communio: Church and Papacy in Early Christianity* (Chicago 1972); the German original appeared in *Miscellanea historiae pontificiae* 7 (1943). Y. Congar, in *Le concile et les conciles* (Paris 1960) 300-34; *L'episcopat et et l'église universelle* (Paris 1962) 227-60—to mention but two of Congar's works in this area. J. Lecuyer, *Etudes sur la collégialité épiscopale* (Paris 1964). M.-J. Le Guillou, *Mission et unité; Les exigences de la communion* (Paris 1960). J. Hamer, *L'église est une communion* (Paris 1962); J. Ratzinger, *Das neue Volk Gottes: Entwürfe zur Ekklesiologie* (Düsseldorf 1969) especially 121-224.

13 Printed with supporting documents in *Papal Primacy and the Universal Church*, ed P. Empie and T. A. Murphy (Minneapolis, MN 1974).

14 Cf. "L'autorité dans l'Eglise," *Irénikon* 50 (1977) 59-68.

15 Ed J. McCord (New York 1976).

16 Pp 16-17.

17 P 16.

18 In *One in Christ* 6 (1970) 101-22.

19 On the close relationship between the words *koinônia* and *metalêpsis* see Elert, 27-8.

20 "Apostolic Continuity and Orthodox Theology: Towards a Synthesis of Two Perspectives," *St Vladimir's Theological Quarterly* 19 (1975) 75-108, now included in *Being as Communion*, 171-208.

21 *Magn.* 6:1, 3:1-2; *Tral.* 3:1.

22 *Ep.* 69 (66):5, 43 (40):5; *De unitate* 4.

23 Exposed by F. Dvornik, *The Idea of Apostolicity in Byzantium and the Legend of the Apostle Andrew* (Cambridge, MA 1958).

24 "Dialogue with Morosini," ed A. Heisenberg, *Neue Quellen zur Geschichte des lateinischen Kaisertums und der Kirchenunion* II (Sitzungsberichte der Bayrischen Akademie der Wissenschaften, Philos., philol. und hist. Klasse, 2. Abh., München 1923) 22.

25 G. Tornikes, "Letter to the Pope in the name of the Emperor," ed J. Darrouzès, *Georges et Démétrios Tornikès: Lettres et discours* (Paris 1970) 326, 332.

26 Cf. Dvornik, *The Idea of Apostolicity*, 163-71. Though the author wishes to demonstrate growing Byzantine awareness of "the importance of apostolic origins" (p 171), the passages which he cites by no means reduce apostolicity to the question of "origins."

27 N. Cabasilas, "On the Primacy of the Pope," PG 149, cols 728D-729A.

28 Cf. the examples given by J. Meyendorff, "St Peter in Byzantine Theology," in *The Primacy of Peter* (London 1963) 10-11.

29 Barlaam of Calabria, quoted by Meyendorff, "St Peter in Byzantine Theology," 23.

30 Ibid.

31 D. Tornikes, "Letter to the Pope in the name of the Patriarch," ed Darrouzès, 351.

32 *Byzantium and the Roman Primacy* (New York 1966).

33 J. Meyendorff, *The Byzantine Legacy in the Orthodox Church* (St Vladimir's Seminary Press, Crestwood, NY 1982) 241.

34 Barlaam of Calabria, quoted by Meyendorff, "St Peter in Byzantine Theology," 21.

35 Balsamon, in Rhalles and Potles, *Syntagma tôn Theiôn kai Hierôn Kanonôn* IV (Athens 1858) 548.

36 Mesarites, ed Heisenberg, 22-3.

37 See especially G. Alberigo, *Lo svillupo della dottrina sui poteri nella Chiesa universale* (Rome 1964), and also the comments of P. Duprey, "Brief Reflections on the Title 'Primus inter pares,'" *One in Christ* 10 (1974) 7-12.

38 On the subject see Bp Pierre (L'Huillier), "Rapport entre pouvoirs d'ordre et de juridiction dans la tradition orientale," *Revue de droit canonique* 23 (1973) 281-9.

39 "On the Primacy of the Pope," PG 149, cols 716AB, 728A.

40 *Cathedra Petri* (Paris 1938) 28; noted by A. Schmemann, "The Idea of Primacy in Orthodox Theology," in *The Primacy of Peter* (London 1963) 49n.

41 The expression is Kallistos Ware's, in "Primacy, Collegiality, and the People of God," *Eastern Churches Review* 3 (1970) 18-29.

42 See, for example, J. Meyendorff, *Living Tradition* (Crestwood, NY 1978) 37: "A conciliar decree needed the 'reception' of the whole Church to be considered a true expression of Tradition. This 'reception,' however, was not a popular referendum or an expression of lay 'democracy' as opposed to clerical 'aristocracy.' It simply implied that no authority suppressed man's freedom to believe or not to believe. Any conciliar decree itself implied the risk of faith, and it was not supposed to suppress this risk in others ..."

43 Acts of the Council of 861, ed W. v. Glanvell, *Die Kanonessammlung des Kardinals Deusdedit* (Paderborn 1905) 607.

44 See above, p 34.
45 "Ecclesiological Awareness," 157.
46 See the comments by A. Dulles, *Models of the Church* (Doubleday, Garden City, NY 1974) 36.
47 Ed J. Darrouzès, *Nicétas Stéthatos: Opuscules et lettres*, Sources Chrétiennes 81 (Paris 1961) 292-365.
48 See A. Pavlov, "Teoriia vostochnogo papisma v novieishei russkoi literature kanonicheskogo prava," *Pravoslavnoe Obozreniie* 1879.
49 Miklosich and Müller, *Acta et diplomata* ... (Vienna 1860) 521.

Chapter 7

The "Autocephalous Church"*

Over the last half century few subjects have provoked so much controversy in the Orthodox world as autocephaly. One need only mention the unedifying disputes between the Russian Orthodox Church and the Patriarchate of Constantinople concerning the status of the churches of Poland, Czechoslovakia and America. Disagreement has centered on the way in which autocephalous status is attained. To put matters in simplest terms, according to the Russian Church, any autocephalous church has the right to grant canonical independence to one of its parts. According to Constantinople, on the other hand, only an ecumenical council can definitively establish an autocephalous church, and any interim arrangements depend upon approbation by Constantinople, acting in its capacity as the "mother church" and "first among equals."[1]

While this debate concerning the granting of autocephaly has proceeded with great acrimony, the nature and content of autocephaly has been left relatively undefined. The word is assumed to have a simple, univocal meaning. In fact, those who use the term often tacitly assume implications which others may not share but which nonetheless color their outlook and at times arouse their emotions.

In present-day Orthodox usage, a church is termed "autocephalous" if it possesses (1) the right to resolve all internal problems on its own authority, independently of all other churches, and (2) the right to appoint its own bishops, among them the head of the church, without

---

* Originally presented as a lecture to the annual Priests' Seminar of the Finnish Orthodox Church, Kuopio, September 1982, incorporating and considerably expanding my article "Autocephaly in Orthodox Canonical Literature to the Thirteenth Century," *St Vladimir's Theological Quarterly* 15 (1971) 28-41.

any obligatory expression of dependence on another church.[2] Similarity between this definition and the definition of internal and external sovereignty given in textbooks on government is hardly coincidental. Autocephaly thus defined in quasi-political terms is seen as arising from a veritable liberation. According to Professor J. Karmires, writing in the Greek *Encyclopedia for Religion and Ethics*: "By this concept [of autocephaly] above all is meant the various local churches that have been emancipated (*kheiraphêto*) and that have their own administrative and spiritual 'head'..."[3] As Professor Karmires immediately goes on to add, these autocephalous churches are also characterized by "the coincidence of their jurisdictional boundaries with those of the corresponding state." Here we have echoes of an idea most forcefully enunciated by Theokletos Pharmakides, principal theoretician of the modern Church of Greece, according to whom independence of a state necessarily implies ecclesiastical independence for the territory of that state. This conception, so well suited to nineteenth-century attitudes toward church/state relations, has continued to influence Orthodox polity in this century. It was used, for example, to justify the autocephaly of the Orthodox church of the new Polish republic following World War I. Usually, however, it has not been the concept of the state as such but rather that of the nation-state that has colored perceptions of autocephaly. To be sure, nationality alone has not completely triumphed as a principle of ecclesiastical organization—witness the fate of the Bulgarian Exarchate in the nineteenth century, when phyletism (tribalism, ethnicism) was officially condemned as a heresy by Constantinople. But nationality linked to statehood has been a very potent force indeed. We find the basic argument expressed in its simplest—and most benign—form by Patriarch Nikon of Moscow in his preface to the 1653 edition of the *Kormchaia Kniga*: though Russia had received Christianity from Constantinople, this did not imply necessary and permanent subordination, "for if a nation has established an independent state not subordinate to the Greek empire, and if that local church gradually has become stronger, it may in time become self-governing in all respects."[4] We find the same argument expressed more stridently in the nineteenth and earlier twentieth century, as the older sense of one Orthodox *oikoumenê* gives way to modern ideas of nationalism and statism.

These are only a few of the elements which may enter into modern definitions of autocephaly. Even from these, one can easily understand why dispassionate discussion of the subject has been so difficult. When reading booklets and articles attacking the autocephaly of the Orthodox Church in America, for example, one often gets the impression that the authors in fact are still battling the ghost of Pharmakides. Unfortunately, the search for an adequate definition of autocephaly is not greatly simplified when one turns from modern church history to the more distant past, for the word "autocephalous" has had a variety of meanings over the centuries.

Autokephalos (lit. "self-headed") is used occasionally by Byzantine writers in the non-technical meaning of "politically independent." Constantine Porphyrogenitus, for example, uses the term to designate the independent city-states of Dalmatia.[5] More frequent is the use of the ecclesiastical term *autokephalos arkhiepiskopos*: a bishop without suffragans, subject directly to a patriarch rather than to the provincial metropolitan. Finally, *autokephalos* is sometimes used in something approaching its current technical meaning, to describe a self-governing, independent ecclesiastical entity. The earliest such use of the word occurs in the *Church History* of Theodore the Reader (ca. 540), where the metropolis of Cyprus is referred to as *autokephalos* and no longer subject to Antioch.[6] Nilus Doxopatres, the twelfth-century ecclesiastical geographer, uses the same adjective when describing the churches of Cyprus and Bulgaria: they are "autocephalous, not subject to any of the greater sees, governing themselves of their own authority and ordaining their own bishops."[7] The same essential characteristic of autocephaly is noted by the great twelfth-century canonist Theodore Balsamon: "formerly all the heads of the provinces were autocephalous and were elected by their respective synods."[8] As understood in the earlier Middle Ages, then, autocephaly consists "precisely and uniquely in the fact that all the bishops of a territory are elected and consecrated by the episcopal college of that territory and that the primate... does not need to receive his investiture from any other primate."[9]

As the quotation from Balsamon suggests, the reality of autocephaly thus defined considerably antedates use of the word "autocephalous." Even before the establishment of Christianity as the favored religion of the state, before structures of coordination were defined in written form by conciliar canons, ecclesiastical organization in the Roman Empire already was modeled along the lines of civil administration. Roughly speaking and with several important exceptions, the churches of each province, headed by the metropolitan (i.e., the bishop of the capital city) and the other bishops, constituted what in effect was an autocephalous unit.[10] They *were* autocephalous; they did not *become* autocephalous nor were they *granted autocephaly* by some higher authority. At the same time, custom, confirmed by conciliar canons from the fourth century onward, had somewhat modified this arrangement. Thus Nicea canon 6 begins:

> Let the ancient customs in Egypt, Libya and Pentapolis prevail, that the Bishop of Alexandria have jurisdiction in all these, since the like is customary for the Bishop of Rome also. Likewise in Antioch and the other provinces, let the churches retain their privileges.[11]

Often interpretations of this canon emphasize the prerogatives of Alexandria, Rome and Antioch as supra-metropolitan powers. It is important, however, to note the context of these words. The two preceding canons both deal with provincial organization and with the prerogatives of metropolitan in particular; and after its initial acknowledgement of certain exceptions arising from "ancient custom," this canon itself immediately continues with further problems of provincial organization:

> And this is to be universally understood, that if anyone be made bishop without the consent of the metropolitan, the great synod has declared that such a man ought not to be a bishop ...

It is also important to recognize the circumstances which produced these "ancient customs." Ecclesiastical organization in Egypt and Italy had not kept pace with the changes in civil administration introduced by the emperor Diocletian toward the end of the third century. As a result, the bishops of Alexandria and Rome were, in effect, metropolitans over several provinces—an anomaly which the council felt obliged to justify. On the other hand, the council apparently did not regard "ancient custom" arising from more strictly religious grounds as sufficient reason to modify their general rule of accommodation to the patterns of civil administration. Thus, while the bishop of Jerusalem is to be honored on account of "custom and ancient tradition," for the time being at least he remains subject to the metropolitan of Caesaria, the civil administrative center (Nicea canon 7).

Concern for maintaining the integrity of provincial organization and authority against encroachment from above is expressed even more forcefully in canon 8 of the Council of Ephesus (431):

> Our brother bishop Rheginus, the beloved of God, and his fellow beloved of God bishops, Zeno and Evagrius, of the province of Cyprus, have reported to us an innovation which has been introduced contrary to the ecclesiastical constitutions and the Canons of the Holy Apostles [canon 35], and which touches upon the liberties of all. Wherefore, since injuries affecting all require the more attention, as they cause the greater damage, and particularly when they are transgressions of an ancient custom; and since those excellent men, who have petitioned the Synod, have told us in writing and by word of mouth that the Bishop of Antioch has in this way held ordinations in Cyprus; therefore the rulers of the holy churches in Cyprus shall enjoy, without dispute or injury, according to the canons of the blessed Fathers and ancient custom, the right of performing for themselves the ordination of their excellent bishops. The same rule shall be observed in the other dioceses and provinces everywhere, so that none of the God-beloved bishops shall assume control of any province which has not heretofore, from the very beginning, been under his own hand or that of his predecessors... Wherefore, this holy and ecumenical Synod has decreed that in every province the rights which heretofore, from the beginning, have belonged to it, shall be preserved to it, according to the old prevailing custom, unchanged and uninjured: every metropolitan having permission to take, for his own security, a copy of these acts. And if any one shall bring forward a rule contrary to what is here determined, this holy and ecumenical Synod unanimously decrees that it shall be of no effect.

This canon, quoted here at length because of its singular interest, often has been interpreted as granting independence to the church of Cyprus, as though Cyprus formerly had been legitimately subject to Antioch.[12] The actual wording of the canon, however, makes it obvious that the council was not *granting* independence to Cyprus but rather was *confirming and preserving* Cyprus' independence against what it regarded as the illegitimate intrusion of Antioch. Indeed the canon expressly attempts to preserve the liberties of all metropolitans and their provincial churches against innovations introduced by the supra-metropolitan powers.

While the Council of Ephesus did succeed in preserving the independence of Cyprus, it did not check the growth of supra-metropolitan organization. Jerusalem, under its ambitious and unscrupulous bishop Juvenal (d. 458), gained supra-metropolitan status over the three provinces of Palestine. Elsewhere in the East, Antioch extended its control on

the basis of canon 6 of Nicea, which by the fifth century was interpreted
as giving that see supra-metropolitan authority throughout the civil diocese of the East. Most spectacular of all was the rise of Constantinople.
Canon 3 of the Council of Constantinople (381) had given that see
simply a vague "prerogative of honor" after Old Rome. Over the next
decades, bishops of Constantinople managed to establish their ascen-
dancy over the three minor civil dioceses of Pontus, Asia and Thrace,
despite the existence of well-established provincial organization and the
manifest absence of "ancient customs" that would justify such developments. At the Council of Chalcedon (451), with the firm support of the
emperor, Archbishop Anatolius of Constantinople gained partial confirmation of the new situation with what has come to be known as canon 28
of that council. While appointment of provincial bishops remains in the
hands of the provincial synod under the metropolitan, the metropolitans
themselves are to be "ordained by the archbishop of Constantinople, after
the proper elections have been held according to custom and have been
reported to him." In addition, "such bishops of the dioceses aforesaid as
are among the barbarians" are to be ordained by him. In effect, the
provinces of the three civil dioceses of Pontus, Asia and Thrace have thus
passed from autocephaly to autonomy, with the archbishop of Constantinople becoming a metropolitan of metropolitans, as it were.[13]

In little more than a hundred years, the structural arrangements envi-
sioned by the fathers of Nicea have been transformed into a system of five
large ecclesiastical divisions headed by the bishops of Rome, Constantinople, Alexandria, Antioch and Jerusalem. But with this "pentarchy" we are
still far from our modern system of autocephalous churches. These large
ecclesiastical divisions are all part of one universal Roman empire; their
existence obviously is not linked to the political independence of the
corresponding civil divisions or to nationality. The very word *ethnos*
(nation) is used simply as a synonym for province, with none of its
modern connotations (Apostolic Canon 34). I have deliberately avoided
referring to these large ecclesiastical divisions as patriarchates because (1)
in this period the word "patriarchate" is rarely used in this context, and
(2) there is little suggestion that these divisions were regarded as modern
patriarchates are: as quasi-sovereign entities. In fact even the term "patriarch" is used in its modern sense, as a uniform designation for the heads

of these divisions, for the first time only by Justinian in the sixth century. Generally other titles were used: in Rome and Alexandria, "pope"; in Antioch, "archbishop" or "exarch"; in Constantinople, "archbishop." Thus, when a writer or speaker referred to the "church of Constantinople" he did not mean the "patriarchate of Constantinople" understood as the combined territories of Pontus, Asia and Thrace, as distinct from the "patriarchate of Jerusalem" or the "patriarchate of Antioch," comprising the three provinces of Palestine and the diocese of the East respectively. He meant Constantinople as distinct from Sardis or Caesarea or Hippo Regius. That church enjoyed a number of privileges, prerogatives and rights, but other churches might have distinct privileges, prerogatives and rights of their own. Rome sent the pallium to metropolitan archbishops throughout much of the West; the pope of Alexandria was preceded on formal occasions by a certain number of taper-bearers... The list of these privileges, prerogatives and rights is virtually endless. They might arise in various ways: by "custom and ancient tradition" in the case of the older apostolic churches, but also by imperial rescript or by the decision of a council of the imperial church (i.e., an ecumenical council). Whatever their source, they seem to have been avidly sought and jealously guarded.

So far we have considered in detail only the right to appoint bishops and metropolitans; and, as we have seen, the right to do this without any obligatory expression of dependence on another ecclesiastical authority was regarded as the essential element of autocephaly. In the period that we are considering, this right remained distinct from another important right which we today also often associate with autocephaly: the right to resolve disputes, and specifically to hear appeals. Particularly in the fourth century, as the Arian controversy unsettled church life, disputes quickly moved beyond the provincial level. Mechanisms for resolving them were urgently needed and had to be quickly improvised. These had no necessary relation to the emerging mechanisms for the regulation of ordinations. According to canon 14 of the Council of Antioch (341):

> If any bishop shall be tried on any accusations, and it should then happen that the bishops of the province disagree concerning him, some pronouncing the accused innocent, and others guilty; for the settlement of all disputes, the holy synod decrees that the metropolitans call on some others belonging to the neighboring province, who shall add their judgement and resolve the dispute, and thus, with those of the province, confirm what is determined.

The famous "appeal canons" of Sardica (343), confirmed by imperial rescripts of 382 and 445, provided a more elaborate way of dealing with the same situation: in certain circumstances the Roman pontiff could review a case, summon a new tribunal from the bishops of the neighboring provinces, and if necessary send presbyters *a latere* to participate in such tribunals (canons 3, 4 and 5). A council in Constantinople in 382 modified the provisions of the Council of Antioch slightly: the larger tribunal including neighboring bishops should be composed of bishops from the same civil diocese.[14] An imperial edict of 421 introduced a further modification by permitting appeal to Constantinople from Pontus, Asia, Thrace, Illyricum and the East (i.e., from a far greater area than was later to comprise the "patriarchate" of Constantinople); and this option was given ecclesiastical recognition by canons 9 and 17 of the Council of Chalcedon (451): those having a difference with their metropolitans may have "recourse to the exarch of the diocese or to the throne of the imperial city of Constantinople."

Of course, these provisions for appeal to Constantinople were made above all because of the presence in Constantinople of the *synodos endêmousa*. This synod was not yet the chief governing body of the "patriarchate" of Constantinople, comprised of the ranking metropolitans of Pontus, Asia and Thrace and subordinate to the archbishop of the capital. Rather, it was still a fluid body sometimes including representatives from the distant East or Illyricum. As such, as the edict of 421 recognized, it was an appropriate substitute for an ecumenical council in handling disciplinary matters.[15]

The Germanic invasions in the West and the rise of Monophysitism and the Arab conquests in the East brought important changes in ecclesiastical geography. The imperial church—effectively reduced to one great see, Constantinople—entered a period of centralization. Rome, shorn of the Greek-speaking provinces of Sicily and southern Italy, was left to its own devices; and Alexandria, Antioch and Jerusalem were nearly forgotten. Whatever pragmatic basis the "pentarchy of patriarchates" may have had in the age of Justinian as a system for church organization was lost. Nevertheless, the theory of the pentarchy gained new strength, particularly in times of theological controversy. To combat imperial interference in dogmatic matters, churchmen like St Theodore of Studios argued that such authority lies with the whole Church as represented by all five patriarchs.[16] With time this theory gained quasi-theological status. Typical is a letter of Peter of Antioch (1054), chiding Peter of Grado for employing the title of patriarch:

> The body of a man is ruled by one head, but in it there are many members, all of which are governed by only five senses ... So also the Body of Christ—that is, the Church of the faithful—made up of diverse nations or members and governed in the same way by five senses—by the five great sees mentioned earlier—is ruled by one head, Christ Himself. And just as no senses other than the five senses exist, so also no patriarch of any sort other than the five patriarchs is allowed.[17]

In Byzantium's golden age the pentarchy thus comes to represent the ideal church order: an ideal of harmony, mutual support, coordination, and—above all—consensus. It is not surprising, therefore, that appeals to pentarchic theory are prominent in twelfth-century Byzantine diatribes against the Roman understanding of primacy: Rome indeed possessed some unique privileges and prerogatives, yet neither Rome nor any other single see could claim full authority to the exclusion of the others.

Despite the ascendence of pentarchic theory through the twelfth century, in practice there were already several exceptions—local churches other than the five patriarchates with the right to appoint all their own bishops. The exceptional status of one such church, that of Cyprus, might be explained by a "pentarchist" as dependent upon the explicit approval of an ecumenical council; however, several other such exceptions existed, especially on the fringes of the empire. Foundations for the autocephaly of Georgia, for example, were laid in the fifth century when, in return for a political alliance and acceptance of his *Henotikon,* the emperor Zeno recognized the catholicos of the Georgian Church as autocephalous, though still vaguely affiliated with Antioch. At the beginning of the seventh century the Georgian Church returned to Chalcedonian orthodoxy but retained its exceptional status, and by the eighth century it was fully independent.[18]

Imperial commands effected the creation of two additional autocephalous churches. In 666 Emperor Constans II issued a *privilegium* to the archbishop of Ravenna and to the appropriate civil authorities declaring the church of Ravenna to be autocephalous. By 677, however, Ravenna's metropolitans were again obliged to seek consecration at Rome; and, because of the ephemeral character of Ravenna's autocephaly, the case did not enter into the "memory" of the Church.[19] Of far greater consequence for the Orthodox canonical tradition is the case of Justiniana Prima. To honor the place of his birth, the emperor Justinian in 535 issued a *novella* granting to the archbishop of Justiniana Prima virtually patriarchal jurisdiction over much of the Balkan peninsula,

> so that the present most holy head of our native place, Justiniana Prima, might be not just a metropolitan ... but an archbishop and that other provinces might be under his authority ... that your beatitude and all the heads of the church of Justiniana Prima shall have the rank of archbishop and enjoy the prerogatives, the power, and the authority over other bishops which that titles gives: that your holiness shall ordain them; that you shall have the highest sacerdotal dignity in the above-mentioned provinces; that this high dignity and these great honors shall be inherent in your see; that these provinces shall have no other archbishop; and that you in no way shall be dependent upon the archbishop of Thessalonika ... When, however, your holiness departs from this life, your successor shall be ordained by the venerable council of the metropolitans of your see ...[20]

The terms of this *novella*, reiterated in *Novella* 131, clearly describe what today would be termed an autocephalous church, even though the word "autocephalous" itself is not used; and although the very location of Justiniana Prima was soon forgotten as a result of the seventh-century Slavic invasions, this legislation concerning the see continued to play an important role in the ecclesiastical politics of the Balkan peninsula throughout the Middle Ages.

During the period of the first Bulgarian empire Byzantium occasionally recognized the existence of an independent Bulgarian patriarchate, but this was due to expediency rather than to an application of the terms of Justinian's *novella*, a *de facto* recognition rather than one *de jure*. The situation changed, however, following the destruction of the independent Bulgar state by Emperor Basil II in 1014. Although the Bulgarian primate, John of Ochrid, was compelled to exchange the title of patriarch for that of archbishop, a series of imperial *novellae* confirmed to him the same jurisdiction which he had formerly possessed.[21] On the death of Basil (1025) John was replaced by a Greek, and increasingly Greeks came to dominate the higher clergy. Yet, almost paradoxically, the chief pursuit of the Greek archbishops of Ochrid was the defense of the ancient privileges of their see against the encroachments of Constantinople. For example,

Theophylact of Ochrid (ca. 1075), a former cleric of Hagia Sophia, at one point complains:

> Why is the patriarch of Constantinople participating in the affairs of the Bulgars, since he does not have the right to select or ordain their autocephalous archbishop nor does he have any other privileges among them?[22]

Similarly John Comnenus, nephew of Emperor Alexius I, resurrected for himself the title of Archbishop of Justianiana Prima (ca. 1143).[23]

Ochrid's vigorous defense of the privileges of Justiniana Prima, along with the continuing existence of autocephalous churches in Cyprus and Georgia, is significant for Byzantium's twelfth-century golden age of canonical thought if only because commentators on ecclesiastical organization felt obliged at least to mention such anomalies. Sometimes these autocephalous churches receive only grudging attention. In his treatise on ecclesiastical geography (1143), Nilus Doxopatres devotes a meager paragraph each to the churches of Cyprus and Bulgaria and then with a note of impatience announces: "And so much for these"; and immediately he continues with an exposition of the mystical significance of the pentarchy, the five senses of Christ's single head, instituted by the Holy Spirit Himself.[24] Professional canonists, on the other hand, devote somewhat more attention to these exceptional cases. Balsamon, for example, offers a stimulating account of the origins of these churches:

> Note from the present canon that once all metropolitans of the provinces were autocephalous and were ordained by their local synods. This, however, has been changed by canon 28 of the Council of Chalcedon, which determined that the metropolitans of the dioceses of Pontus, Asia and Thrace along with a few others mentioned in that canon were to be ordained by the patriarch of Constantinople and subject to him. But if you find yet other autocephalous churches, like that of Bulgaria, that of Cyprus, and that of Iberia [i.e., Georgia], do not be surprised. For Emperor Justinian honored the archbishop of Bulgaria ... The third synod [i.e., the Council of Ephesus] honored the archbishop of Cyprus ... Likewise a decision of an Antiochian synod honored the archbishop of Iberia. For it was said that at the time of the most holy patriarch of the city of God great Antioch, lord Peter, there was a synodal arrangement that the church of Iberia, then subject to the patriarch of Antioch, should be free and autocephalous.[25]

While Balsamon's account does not entirely accord with subsequent historical scholarship,[26] his basic position is clear. Autocephaly—and for that matter virtually every other aspect of supra-episcopal organization—

is established by means of legal acts, whether decision of an ecumenical council or arrangement of the mother church or imperial decree.

This pragmatic view of ecclesiastical organization can be found in Balsamon's discussion of the patriarchates as well. The church of Jerusalem, for example, had been founded by St James;[27] nevertheless it was subject to the metropolitan of Caesarea until I Nicea canon 7 honored it on account of Christ's death and resurrection.[28] Even the church of Rome, though founded by St Peter,[29] owed its prerogatives and privileges to the decisions of ecumenical councils (e.g., I Nicea canon 6) and above all to the so-called *Donation of Constantine*.[30] Constantinople, on the other hand, could claim no illustrious founder;[31] but because it was the imperial city, I Constantinople canon 3 and Chalcedon canon 28 had conferred on it all the privileges possessed by Old Rome, including those conveyed by the *Donation of Constantine*.[32]

Balsamon has little use for the more metaphysical aspects of pentarchic theory or for any other purely theological approach to church order. While he devotes an entire treatise to describing and defining the powers and prerogatives of the five patriarchates, he is relatively uninterested in their mystical or symbolical significance. Rather, for Balsamon, patriarchates, primacies, special prerogatives and other aspects of supra-episcopal organization are established by means of legal acts, which in turn have been framed in response to various special circumstances—above all, political circumstances. Time and again Balsamon points out that Constantinople, like Rome before it, was honored because it is the imperial city.

Balsamon's typically Byzantine preference for the stipulations of the *ius scriptum* of course is quite different from the early Church's sensitivity to "ancient custom and tradition." At the same time, his awareness of the importance of political circumstances for ecclesiastical organization is part of a long tradition, written and unwritten, of accommodation to the patterns of civil administration. Yet there are dangers in too closely linking ecclesiastical organization to the whims of secular politics. Already in the fourth century St Basil the Great had to deal with the arbitrary division of provinces by civil decree,[33] and in the following century Chalcedon canon 12 touched upon the same issue. Balsamon too is aware of such dangers and tries to provide a measure of stability by stressing the legal acts requisite for effecting any changes in a church's status. More specifically, he invokes canon 37 of the Synod in Trullo (692), which preserves the rights and status of bishops unable to enter their dioceses on account of barbarian incursions. It is principally on these grounds that he defends the prerogatives of the patriarchates which have fallen into the hostile hands of the Latins, his own see of Antioch among them.[34] Unfortunately for the history of Orthodox canon law, Balsamon did not live long enough to comment on the full range of ecclesiastical problems which can arise from complete disruption of political circumstances. In 1204, within a decade of his death, a western crusading army captured Constantinople itself, making it the capital of a Latin empire. Hard upon this political collapse came ecclesiastical chaos.

With the Latin conquest, the remnants of Byzantine ecclesiastical and political organization were placed in an awkward position. On the one hand, the importance of the imperial will and presence for ecclesiastical organization had always been recognized in Byzantium. But where was the empire now? Several Greek successor states had been established on former imperial territory, but none possessed unquestioned legitimacy of dynasty, preponderance of physical power, or (most importantly) the imperial city of Constantinople. On the other hand, crowning by the patriarch had come to be considered essential to the making of an emperor. But now a Latin was enthroned as patriarch in Constantinople, and the pre-1204 patriarch, John X Camaterus, had taken refuge in Bulgaria, pointedly ignoring invitations to the court of Nicea, the leading Greek successor state. Byzantium's delicate balance of church and empire had degenerated into a frustrating state of paralysis. Disputes over ecclesiastical jurisdiction raged but achieved no definitive resolution, at least on the level of theory. Many central canonical questions were raised but left unanswered—or else left with too many answers. Detailed investigation of the ecclesiastical politics of this period would be out of place at this point,[35] but a brief sketch of some of the canonical issues involved perhaps will suggest some of the reasons why autocephaly, comparatively clearly defined in earlier periods, now comes to be a subject for debate and confusion.

The initiative in restoring the forms of the old Byzantine court was taken by Theodore I Lascaris of Nicea. Patriarch John Camaterus, who had rejected Lascaris' overtures, died in 1206, and the patriarchal throne remained vacant until 1208. Then, after winning the support of most of the Anatolian metropolitans, Lascaris arranged for the appointment of Michael Autoreianus as patriarch. Immediately thereafter Autoreianus crowned Lascaris emperor. Thus, by a kind of *allêlogenesis*, a Greek emperor and patriarch now held court in Nicea. Needless to say, the other Greek states were not quick to accept these new arrangements.

Autoreianus and his successors appear to have enjoyed considerable authority even in areas beyond the political control of Nicea. Greeks remaining in Latin-occupied Constantinople eventually looked to them for guidance;[36] a patriarch of Antioch and his colleagues sought absolution after having submitted to the Pope;[37] the bishops of Cyprus requested confirmation for their new archbishop's election;[38] Armenians and Latins discussed possible church union;[39] Russians corresponded ...[40] At the same time, the patriarchs were utterly dedicated to the Nicene cause, and as a result their claims to jurisdiction were vigorously resisted in the other Greek successor states.

In distant Trebizond, where David and Alexius Comnenus, grandsons of Emperor Andronicus I, had established a little empire, the local metropolitan became in practice autocephalous. Ecclesiastical relations with the patriarch at Nicea were restored only in 1260, when Patriarch Nicephorus II, to assure Trebizond's cooperation in Emperor Michael VIII Palaeologus' coming campaign to recapture Constantinople, recognized the church of Trebizond's right to handle all its own internal affairs and to appoint its own bishops and metropolitans on the condition that a representative of the patriarch of Constantinople be present at the consecration of the metropolitan of Trebizond.[41] A similar pattern was followed in Epirus, where Michael Ducas and Theodore Comnenus Ducas were proving worthy rivals of Nicea's Lascarids. Metropolitans like John Apocaucus of Naupactus, ignoring the claims of Nicea's patriarchs, assumed control of stauropegiac monasteries (monasteries subject directly to the patriarch rather than to the local bishop) and proceeded with the ordination of bishops and fellow-metropolitans.

The protracted ecclesiastical and political duel between Nicea and Epirus took a new turn in 1219, when Nicea's Patriarch Germanus II consecrated Sava, saintly son of the king of Serbia, as autocephalous archbishop of Serbia. Since the six ecclesiastical provinces comprising the Serbian church until this point had been under the jurisdiction of the autocephalous archbishop of Ochrid, the canonicity of the consecration was immediately questioned. In angry letters to the patriarch and to the "monk Sava," Demetrius Chomatianus—archbishop of Ochrid, distinguished canonist and partisan of the despotate of Epirus—claimed that the consecration violated I Constantinople canon 2, Apostolic canon 35 and Antioch canon 13 (all directed against bishops performing ordinations outside their own jurisdiction), Chalcedon canon 12 (against setting up two metropolitans within the same province by recourse to the civil authorities) and Ephesus canon 8 (defense of the church of Cyprus against interference by the patriarch of Antioch).[42]

Needless to say, the canonical merits of Chomatianus' position were ignored both in Serbia and in Nicea. Soon, however, Chomatianus was able to even the score. In 1224 Theodore Comnenus Ducas, Despot of Epirus, captured Thessalonica from the Latins, proving that his state was a serious contender in the race to recapture Constantinople and restore the empire. Theodore's ambitions were literally crowned by Chomatianus, who crowned and anointed him emperor in direct opposition to the claims of Nicea's Lascarids. As one might expect, Patriarch Germanus II questioned the legality of Chomatianus' act: Since when has the archbishop of Bulgaria had the right to crown emperors? How does a cleric of Ochrid dare to extend a patriarchal right hand to anoint an imperial forehead? And how could he arrogate to himself the patriarchal right to bless the *myron* (chrism) used for that anointing?[43] In reply, Chomatianus argued that as head of the autocephalous church of Justiniana Prima he could anoint emperors whomever, wherever and however he wished, for neither the anointing of emperors nor the confection of *myron* was the exclusive prerogative of the patriarch.[44] To be sure—Chomatianus admits—I have had to accommodate myself to the circumstances, convinced that it was preferable to adjust to the times rather than follow the law's precision. But wasn't this also the case when an emperor and a patriarch were proclaimed in Nicea? After all, whoever has heard of one and the same person shepherding the metropolis of Nicea and at the same time being called patriarch of Constantinople? Those who survived the holocaust of the Latin conquest did not go only to Nicea to proclaim an emperor. Many have also come to the west (i.e., Greece), where they too have proclaimed an emperor. In view of such radically changed circumstances, Patriarch Germanus at the very least should allow the westerners to manage their own affairs and be satisfied with managing the affairs of Anatolia.[45]

Epirus's triumph was short-lived. In 1230 Theodore was decisively defeated in battle, captured and blinded by the Bulgarian czar, John II Asen. Though the Epirote state survived, it no longer was a serious contender for Constantinople, and in its place Nicea was able to assert its authority in matters ecclesiastical as well as political. As a sign of the changing times, a patriarchal exarch visited Epirus in 1232. Metropolitan John Apocaucus, leader of Epirote ecclesiastical separatism, was forced to retire to a monastery. Chomatianus retained his see, and Ochrid remained autocephalous, but its importance and geographic extent were considerably diminished. Even before the Serbian church withdrew from Ochrid's jurisdiction, the church of the revived Bulgarian empire, likewise made up of provinces formerly under Ochrid's jurisdiction, had become *de facto* autocephalous under its own patriarch at Trnovo; and in 1235, ignoring Ochrid's claims, the patriarch of Constantinople at Nicea, along with the other eastern patriarchs, had granted official recognition to this new patriarchate.

After the fall of Epirus, Nicea's emperors and patriarchs had no serious rivals in the Greek world. The jurisdictional chaos of the period 1204-30 effectively came to an end; and after Constantinople was recaptured from the Latins (1261), emperor and patriarch moved from Nicea back to the imperial city, restoring some semblance of the *status quo ante*. Since 1204, however, a number of changes had taken place in ecclesiastical organization, seriously affecting the meaning of "autocephaly." If nothing else, ecclesiastical geography was different. In addition to the autocephalous churches described by Balsamon—Ochrid, Cyprus, Georgia—there now existed an autocephalous Serbian church under the archbishop of Pec and an autocephalous Bulgarian church under the patriarch of Trnovo.

These two churches possessed a number of features in common which distinguished them from earlier autocephalous churches and at the same time anticipated those of modern times. At least at the time of their establishment, the autocephalous churches of Justiniana Prima and

Cyprus—and indeed the five ancient patriarchates as well—were part of one empire and received legal confirmation of their status by the unilateral decree of an emperor or an ecumenical council. The new foundations, on the other hand, came into existence as one aspect of bilateral treaties between two civil governments, reflecting a tendency to regard autocephaly chiefly as the sign of an independent national state. Thus the patriarchate of Bulgaria was sanctioned as part of a "package deal" which also called for alliance against the Latin emperor and the marriage of Theodore Lascaris' son to the daughter of the Bulgarian czar. Similar political considerations entered into the establishment of the Serbian church. Whereas autocephaly formerly had meant independence on a strictly ecclesiastical level, now it meant political independence, expressed above all in the right to consecrate the *myron* needed for anointing an emperor. As one curious result of this virtual redefinition of terms, autocephaly increasingly became (at least by the standards of previous centuries) conditional and partial, limited by treaty and juridically revokable. For example, in exchange for autocephaly the Serbian and Bulgarian churches both agreed to commemorate the patriarch of Constantinople first in the liturgy and—at least in the case of Bulgaria—to pay him an annual tax.[46]

Another feature peculiar to these new autocephalous churches is that ecclesiastical recognition of their status came in the first instance from the patriarch of Constantinople. Balsamon, at this point representative of the earlier canonical tradition, had recognized that churches can become autocephalous in a variety of ways and attributed no special prerogatives to Constantinople in this regard. Now, however, as the question of autocephaly became so deeply entangled in the immediate political situation of rivalry between Nicea and Epirus, the claims of the "mother church"—Ochrid—were ignored, and the authority of Constantinople was extended. To be sure, one element in earlier ecclesiology seems to have been maintained at least for a time: the ideal of consensus represented by the pentarchy. St Sava's archepiscopal consecration may very well have taken place as churchmen from far and wide gathered in Nicea in 1220 for the pan-Orthodox synod which Theodore Lascaris had called in order to discuss possible negotiations with Rome.[48] Better substantiated is the involvement of the patriarchs of Alexandria, Antioch and

Jerusalem in the decision to recognize the Bulgarian church as an auto-cephalous patriarchate.[48] Yet in these episodes the image of the pentarchy seems to be fading, while that of the patriarch of Constantinople is growing ever sharper. In the next generation, for example, in Domentijan's *Life of St Sava*, the patriarch is described as "the father of the fathers of the whole *oikoumenê*," who gives to the new archbishop—"his newly born son"—all the insignia of office and enjoins all Orthodox Christians to heed him even as they would heed the patriarch himself.[49] In short, already in the thirteenth century we have intimations of a view of patriarchal authority which will become especially prominent in the fourteenth century—a view epitomized in Patriarch Philotheus Coccinus' famous letter to the Russian princes:

> Since God has appointed Our Humility as leader of all Christians found anywhere in the *oikumenê*, as protector and guardian of their souls, all of them depend on me, the father and teacher of them all. If that were possible, therefore, it would have been my duty to walk throughout the cities and countries everywhere on earth and teach in them the Word of God, doing so unfailingly, since such is our duty. But since it is beyond the capacity of one weak and helpless man to walk around the entire *oikoumenê*, Our Humility chooses the best among men, the most eminent in virtue, and sends them to the ends of the universe. One of them goes to your country, to the multitudes which inhabit it, another reaches other areas of the earth, and still another goes elsewhere, so that each, in the country and place appointed to him, enjoys territorial rights and episcopal see, and all the rights of Our Humility.[50]

Here a minor episode perhaps deserves mention. Early in the dispute between Epirus and Nicea, Metropolitan John Apocaucus received a letter in which his adversary added the words "ecumenical patriarch" to his signature. This provoked Apocaucus to observe that never in his long years at the offices of the patriarchate in Constantinople had he encountered such a thing.[51] This assertion at first glance seems implausible, for as is well known the title "ecumenical patriarch" goes back to the sixth century.[52] Yet in the twelfth century it appears not to have been used very often, at least not in official signatures. In the thirteenth, however, it is used very frequently both in official documents and elsewhere. For example, in his *Life of St Sava* Domentijan uses the title at every possible opportunity. It is as though the patriarch has replaced the emperor and empire as focus of the *oikoumenê*, as symbol of the unity of the Orthodox Christian world. While the empire itself has shrunk to a shadow of its old self, patriarchs like Germanus II with some justice can boast of their pastoral authority bearing fruit among the inhabitants of the Crimea, the Armenians and Georgians, the Russians, and the Melkites of Jerusalem. And as these patriarchs rebut papal claims to universal authority, a new element can be found alongside old appeals to the pentarchy—appeals to the numerous nations who feel as the Greeks do, the Ethiopians and the Syrians of the interior, the Iberians, the Abasges, the Alans, the Goths, the Khazars, Russia with its thousands of tribes, the kingdom of the Bulgars, rich in victories …[53]

In the thirteenth century, a new sense of universalism is emerging, but at the same time, a new sense of nationalism. This is most obvious in the establishment of the new Bulgarian and Serbian autocephalies. The bishops consecrated by St Sava for his new church were Serbs as distinct from Greeks, and in places like Ras where there was a Greek incumbent, he was ousted—to the consternation of Demetrius Chomatianus.[54] A similar sense of national identity can be seen in some Greek circles in this period—a circumstance which helps to explain the pathos of the ecclesiastical dispute between Epirus and Nicea. If it was fitting for the Serbs and the Bulgars to have their own church and their own state, why was this not also the case for the western Greeks? This seems to have been the line of reasoning taken by John Apocaucus and Demetrius Chomatianus. They did not claim to be universal. They were willing to acknowledge the authority of the patriarch in his own sphere and even to commemorate him first in the liturgy. But they refused to recognize Theodore Lascaris as universal emperor. He was simply the ruler at Nicea, they in the west having their own state. But at Nicea such an approach to political and ecclesiastical life was out of the question.[55] In the eyes of Nicea at least, autocephaly for the western Greeks was as unthinkable as autocephaly for the Bulgars and Serbs was natural. There could be but one Greek state and church.

In the course of these thirteenth-century disputes, autocephaly assumes an *ad hoc* quality less affected by the Church's earlier canonical tradition than by the political exigencies of the moment. In part this is because the parties involved were not above juggling the canons to suit their own private ends; but it is also because the canons themselves, for the most part products of and predicated upon the existence of one

Christian empire, failed to provide consistent and unequivocal answers to the problems of the day. The eventual political and military triumph of Nicea, by restoring the empire, provided a respite from the jurisdictional chaos and assured continuation—and indeed expansion—of the authority of the patriarch of Constantinople, New Rome. But the canonical problems raised by the collapse of empire remained, and still remain, unsolved.

*   *   *   *

This historical investigation of "autocephaly" should dispel at least one common misconception. Very often autocephaly is taken to be a univocal, self-evident and utterly fundamental principle of Orthodox ecclesiology, as though the notion of autocephaly has remained—and will forever remain—consistent and unchanged. But as we have seen, forms of supra-episcopal organization in Orthodoxy have in fact varied considerably. In antiquity each province in effect constituted an autocephalous church. In the imperial period there was a marked tendency to centralization, first into patriarchates and then around a single center, Constantinople. But in the twentieth century we have entered a new period in the history of ecclesiastical organization, one in which we can no longer appeal to this or that isolated historical precedent.

Here, by way of example, the situation of Orthodoxy in America could be noted. As indicated at the beginning of this essay, the patriarchate of Moscow seems to take as axiomatic the principle that any autocephalous church has the right to grant autocephaly to one of its parts, and on this basis it recognized as autocephalous its former North American mission, now the Orthodox Church in America (OCA). The patriarchate of Constantinople has vigorously protested this autocephaly, arguing that only an ecumenical council can definitively establish an autocephalous church and that any interim arrangements depend above all upon approbation by Constantinople. Now the approach of Moscow certainly is consistent with nineteenth-century ideas which would regard the auto-cephalous church as the spiritual counterpart of the sovereign nation-state, and the approach of Constantinople is consistent with the "newer tomes of autocephaly" to which it so often refers, even though this clearly ignores much of the historical evidence presented here. Yet in their official pronouncements neither Moscow nor Constantinople take into consideration all the dimensions of the actual American situation. Moscow has tried to ignore the multitude of overlapping ethnic jurisdictions in America or at most has regarded them as regrettable anomalies, while Constantinople has failed to recognize the existence, growth and vitality—or even the possibility—of authentic church life that is at once both Orthodox and American. As a result, their debate over "who has the right to grant autocephaly" has been sterile, without possibility of resolution.

In all this controversy, one should also note the lack of correspondence between spiritual content and canonical forms, so that the very same church may be regarded by one party as autocephalous and by another as autonomous or possibly even as completely uncanonical. Authentic church life may be present yet still be ignored or mislabeled. Conversely, authentic spiritual life may be absent yet canonical recognition be extended. Thus, as we debate about who has the right to grant autocephaly, as we wait for a Great and Holy Council to answer such questions, in fact we are ignoring the real source of the canonical chaos of our time: that miserable ecclesiological nominalism which ignores spiritual reality in favor of empty names, claims and titles. Should we not instead discuss real issues, however painful this may be? Do we care enough—love enough—to take upon ourselves this cross of truth?

NOTES

1 See the correspondence between Constantinople and Moscow on the subject of the autocephaly of the Orthodox Church in America, collected in *St Vladimir's Theological Quarterly* 15 (1971) 42-80.
2 A. Bogolepov, *Toward an American Orthodox Church* (New York 1963) 15.
3 *S.v. ekklêsia.*
4 Noted by Bogolepov, 18-19.
5 *De administrando imperio* 29, ed G. Moravcsik (Washington 1967) 126.
6 *Excerpta ex ecclesiastica historia* 2.2, PG 86.1, cols 183-4.
7 *Notitia thronorum patriarchalium*, PG 132, col 197.
8 Commentary on I Constantinople canon 2, PG 137, cols 317-8.
9 Bp Pierre (L'Huillier), "Problems Concerning Autocephaly," *Greek Orthodox Theological Review* 24 (1979) 165-91 at p 168.
10 See particularly Antioch canons 8, 9, 11, 13, 15, 19, 10, and I Constantinople canon 2. On this subject of "accommodation" to patterns of civil administration

see F. Dvornik, *The Idea of Apostolicity in Byzantium and the Legend of the Apostle Andrew* (Cambridge, MA 1958) 3-38, and his *Byzantium and the Roman Primacy* (New York 1966), especially 27-39.

11 Here and throughout this essay unless otherwise noted, translations of the ancient conciliar canons are taken from *The Seven Ecumenical Councils, A Select Library of Nicene and Post-Nicene Fathers*, 2nd ser, vol 14, sometimes slightly modified.

12 E.g., by Balsamon. See above p. 101.

13 See especially Bp Pierre (L'Huillier), "Un aspect estompé du 28e canon de Chalcedoine," *Revue de Droit Canonique* 29 (1979) 12-22, and "Le decret du Concile de Chalcedoine sur les prérogatives du siège de la Trés Sainte Église de Constantinople," *Messager de l'Exarchat du Patriarche Russe en Europe Occidentale* nos 101-4 (January-December 1979) 33-69.

14 Usually included in canonical collections as canon 6 of I Constantinople, 381.

15 On the *synodos endêmousa* see the study of I. Hajjar, *Le synode permanent dans l'Église Byzantine des origines au Xeme siècle* (=Orientalia Christiana Analecta 164, Rome 1967).

16 E.g., *Ep.* 124, PG 99, col 1417: "Here we are not discussing secular matters. To judge them is the right of the emperor and the secular tribunal. We are discussing divine and heavenly judgments, and these are committed to no others than those to whom God the Word himself said, 'Whatsoever you shall bind ...' Who are those to whom this mandate was given? To him who holds the throne of Rome, which is the first throne; to him who holds the throne of Constantinople, which is the second; and after them to those who hold the thrones of Alexandria, Antioch and Jerusalem. This is the pentarchic authority of the Church; these have jurisdiction over divine dogmas. It appertains to the emperor and secular authority to give assistance and confirm what has been decided."

17 Ed C. Will, *Acta et scripta quae de controversiis ecclesiae graecae et latinae saeculo undecimo composita extant* (Leipzig 1861) 211-2.

18 On the Georgian Church see especially M. Tarchnishvili, "Die Entstehung und Entwicklung der kirchlichen Autokephalie Georgiens," *Le Muséon* 73 (1960) 107-26, and also J. Dadeshkeliani, "The Autocephaly of the Orthodox Church of Georgia," *The Christian East* 3 (1950) 65-72.

19 F. Dölger, *Regesten* (Corpus der griechischen Urkunden des Mittelalters und der neueren Zeit, Reihe A, Abt. 1) nos 233, 238.

20 *Novella* 11. On the (questionable) medieval identification of Justiniana Prima with Ochrid, see M. J. Zeiller, "Le site de Justiniana Prima," in *Mélanges Charles Diehl* (Paris 1930) vol 1, 299-304.

21 Dölger, *Regesten*, nos 806-8.

22 *Ep.* 27, PG 126, col 428.

23 J. D. Mansi, *Sacrorum Conciliorum Nova et Amplissima Collectio*, vol 21, col 837.

24 *Notitia thronarum patriarchalium*, PG 132, col 1097.

25 Commentary on I Constantinople canon 2, PG 137, cols 317-20.

26 On the question of Georgia's autocephaly, see above at n 18. Balsamon's "Lord Peter" perhaps is Peter the Fuller, monophysite patriarch of Antioch; thus Tarchnishvili, "Die Entstehung ..."

27 *Meditatum de patriarcharum privilegiis*, PG 138, col 1013.

28 Commentary on I Nicea canon 6, PG 137, cols 252-3.

29 *Meditatum* ... PG 138, col 1013.

30 E.g., commentaries on I Constantinople 3, PG 137, col 321 and Antioch canon 12, PG 137, col 1312.

31 *Meditatum* ... PG 138, col 1013. Though Balsamon at this point links St Andrew with Thrace, he does not claim him as founder of the Church of Constantinople, nor does he account St Andrew's disciple Stachys as first bishop of Constantinople. On the legends of the Apostle Andrew see F. Dvornik, *The Idea of Apostolicity...*, especially 138-264.

32 Thus the passages cited above, n 30.

33 Basil the Great, *Ep.* 74-75, cf. Gregory of Nazianzen, *Or.* 43.38.

34 *Meditatum* ... PG 138, col 1032.

35 On the subject see especially D. Nicol, *The Despotate of Epiros* (Oxford 1957) especially 76-102, and A. Karpozilos, *The Ecclesiastical Controversy Between the Kingdom of Nicea and the Principality of Epiros (1217-1233)* (=Byzantine Keimena kai Meletai 7, Thessalonica 1973).

36 See. V. Laurent, *Les Regestes des actes du Patriarcat de Constantinople* 1.4 (Paris 1971) no 1219.

37 *Regestes*, no 1220.

38 *Regestes*, no 1210, cf. 1253.

39 *Regestes*, nos 1224, 1290, 1309, 1313, 1332.

40 *Regestes*, no 1247.

41 On this episode see L. Petit, "Acte synodal du patriarche Nicéphore II sur les privilèges du metropolitan de Trebizonde (1er janvier 1260)," *Izvestiia Russkago Arkheologicheskago Instituta v Konstantinopole* 8 (1902) 163-71.

42 Ed J.-B. Pitra, *Analecta sacra et classica spicilegio solesmense parata* 7 (Rome 1891) 381-90. On the episode see now D. Obolensky's "portrait" of St Sava in *Six Byzantine Portraits* (Clarendon, Oxford 1988), especially 149-53, 158-61.

43 Ibid. 484-5. Concerning the anointing of emperors in Byzantium, see D. Nicol, "Kaisersalbung: The Unction of Emperors in Late Byzantine Coronation Ritual," *Byzantine and Modern Greek Studies* 2 (1976) 37-52, for a relatively recent summing up of the subject, and since then M. Arranz, "L'aspect rituel de

Chapter 8

The Problem of Sacramental "Economy"*

How are non-Orthodox laity or clergy seeking entrance into the Orthodox Church to be received? Such questions cannot be answered simply by describing how these persons are in fact received. Practice in America and elsewhere varies from jurisdiction to jurisdiction and occasionally even within jurisdictions. Thus, for example, depending upon the group or bishop receiving him, a Roman Catholic priest might be (re)baptized, chrismated and ordained; or chrismated and ordained; or chrismated whether wholly or partially and then received in his orders; or received in his orders simply upon profession of the Orthodox faith. Varied also are the theological arguments advanced to justify these various practices. Even when two groups follow the same practice, they may justify it in different ways. For example, most Orthodox these days would receive a non-Chalcedonian or a Roman Catholic or a mainstream Protestant without (re)baptism, and most would receive at least non-Chalcedonian clerics in their orders, without (re)ordination. But how is this reception to be explained? So also, most Orthodox these days would not receive Protestant clergy in their orders. But how is this non-reception to be explained?

Since the time of Peter Moghila in the seventeenth century, many Orthodox theologians would say that non-Chalcedonians, Roman Catholics and mainstream Protestants have a "valid baptism," i.e., baptism in the name of the Trinity, and thus are to be received without rebaptism; but that the Protestants at least do not have "valid orders," whether

* A slightly revised version of a paper presented for discussion at the annual meeting of the Orthodox Theological Society of America, May 1984, and originally printed in *St Vladimir's Theological Quarterly* 29 (1985) 115-32.

because of a break in "apostolic succession" or because of a defect of intention, and thus cannot be received as clerics without ordination. This explanation, of course, depends heavily on Augustine's arguments against the Donatists as developed by the scholastics and codified after Trent. The sacraments are regarded as valid *ex opere operato* if certain objective conditions are met, though this does not necessarily make them licit or fruitful. Thus, while the non-Chalcedonians have "valid orders," they do not have the lawful exercise thereof.

These days this approach to sacramental theology is frequently criticized by Orthodox theologians as hopelessly latinized. At the same time it should be acknowledged that the work of Moghila and his heirs did respond to a definite need. It offered a comprehensive way of accounting for the relation of the sacraments to the Church and hence of explaining the significance of ordination and other sacraments administered outside the Church's canonical limits.

An alternative approach to the question of acceptance or non-acceptance has been particularly prominent in Greek sacramental theology since the eighteenth century. For convenience this approach may be labeled "economic" because of the prominence which it gives to the term *oikonomia* or "economy." While presentations of this economic approach vary considerably in particulars, certain elements are common to most of them:[1]

1. *Oikonomia* is understood as the departure from or suspension of strict application (*akribeia*) of the Church's canons and disciplinary norms, making it in many respects analogous to the West's *dispensatio*.

2. But *oikonomia* is broader than *dispensatio* in that it is not limited to canon law but applies to sacramental theology as well.

3. In this context, from the point of view of *akribeia* all non-Orthodox sacraments are null and void. (Here the East's adherence to a "Cyprianic" ecclesiology is often noted, as distinct from the West's "Augustinian" approach.)

4. But the Orthodox Church, as sole steward of grace, as sovereign administrator of the sacraments, can decide to accept the sacraments of non-Orthodox entering the Church as valid "by economy"—*kat' oikonomian*.

5. This concerns only the sacraments of those entering the Orthodox Church and in no way implies recognition of the validity of non-Orthodox sacraments *per se*.

6. The application of *oikonomia* need not be everywhere and always the same, but may and should change according to the circumstances.

7. These circumstances may include such considerations as (a) the attitude of the non-Orthodox group in question toward Orthodoxy, (b) the spiritual and perhaps also the temporal well-being of the Orthodox flock, (c) the ultimate spiritual well-being of the person or group that contemplates entering the Orthodox Church.

Oikonomia thus understood has found widespread support. Some have found it a welcome panacea for all manner of ecclesiastical ills. In particular, it is seen as a convenient way out of several apparent impasses in ecumenical relations, such as that created by Rome's 1896 rejection of Anglican orders as "absolutely null and utterly void."[2] Others—quite a different group!—have been attracted by its Cyprianic exaltation of the Church as the exclusive vehicle of salvation. For them, outside the canonical limits of the Orthodox Church there is simply undifferentiated darkness, in which rites like baptism and ordination have no more significance than non-baptism and non-ordination. But regardless of such obvious differences in orientation, virtually all proponents of "economy" have claimed that this approach represents the perennial teaching of the Orthodox Church, that it faithfully upholds that understanding of the sacraments and their relationship to the Church which characterized Christian antiquity generally and which has been maintained since then in the East, save where latinization has taken its toll.

A comprehensive evaluation of this claim cannot be undertaken in this brief paper. Here I shall limit myself to the relatively simple task of examining the ways in which the term *oikonomia* was actually used in Byzantine canonical literature, giving particular attention to the question of orders. Yet even this limited examination suggests that the economic approach to sacramental theology lacks historical depth, despite its claims to antiquity. In fact its proponents have formed their "Orthodox concept of sacramental economy" from a few isolated quotations, ignoring or

obscuring the existence and development of specific, well-defined uses of
the term *oikonomia* while at the same time distorting beyond recognition
certain clearly non-technical uses.

Of the meanings of *oikonomia* in Byzantium, the most obvious one
is the one most often ignored by proponents of the economic approach
to sacramental theology: management, arrangement, determination, in
a strictly neutral sense. In canonical texts the term frequently refers to
an arrangement or determination made by a synod of bishops, to the
"handling" of a particular problem. Above all, it refers to a bishop's
management or administration of his diocese, or to particular instances
of this. For the good Byzantine bishop, as seen not just in hortatory
treatises and hagiography but also in routine documents relating to
church affairs, was above all an *oikonomos* : a manager, a steward. To be
sure, financial affairs were entrusted to a professional—this the Council
of Chalcedon had insisted upon many centuries before (canon 26). But
the bishop was still the *oikonomos tês arkhieratikos kharitos,* as the
ordination prayer put it, the steward or manager of the high-priestly
grace, responsible for the pastoral care of his flock, the supervision of his
church's sacramental life.

The most frequently encountered technical use of the word *oikonomia*
in canonical literature reflects this pastoral orientation:[3] the apportion-
ment or disposition of a penance. Here considerable administrative discretion was demanded, for the ancient canons on the subject often
seemed wooden, insensitive. Yet the *oikonomia* of penance was not to
become capricious or arbitrary. Rather, it was to be based upon an
objective diagnosis of the sinner's spiritual malady. Given his condition in
life, the circumstances of his sin and—above all—his zeal for repentance,
what is the appropriate course of treatment?

No doubt it is fortunate that in these penitential matters, as in financial affairs, the bishop had some professional assistance. Cases involving a
public offense might be dealt with by the bishop himself, but for the most
part penance was administered by specially licensed confessors, generally
hieromonks distinguished by their spiritual insight, but even more by the
fact that "they knew the remedies,"[4] they were "experts in the science of
spiritual medicine."[5] The reconciliation of heretics, however, was generally the bishop's task. Their conversion, according to the canons and the

civil law, was to be his constant concern. But how were they to be received? At first glance, the relevant canons presented certain difficulties in interpretation. The age-old practice of the church of Constantinople, as set forth in a number of canonical and liturgical texts, distinguished between heretics who were to be received as heathens (i.e., baptized) and those to be received by anointing with chrism or simply by confession of faith.[6] On the other hand the Apostolic Canons categorically rejected heretic baptism (canons 46, 47), and Cyprian, whose baptismal council of 257 AD was included among the canons, prescribed (re)baptism for all those not baptized within the bosom of the one Church, not only all heretics but schismatics as well.

The problem of harmonizing these texts arose from time to time. In the course of the moechian (adultery) controversy, Naucratius questioned his master Theodore the Studite on this very point, presumably because it seemed odd not to insist on rebaptism of those baptized by the moechians, if, as Theodore insisted, they were truly heretics. Though his contemporaries might accuse him of "Cyprianizing,"[7] Theodore here shows no inclination to put Cyprian's ideas on baptism into practice. Naucratius had said that the Apostolic Canon "by no means makes distinctions, but rather definitively declares that those who are ordained or baptized by heretics are neither clerics nor Christians." But take note, says Theodore, that the Apostolic Canon calls "heretics" those who are not baptized and do not baptize in the name of the Trinity. St Basil, he continues, teaches the same thing. He calls "heretics" those wholly cut off and estranged with respect to the faith itself. These he distinguishes from "schismatics," whose separation can be remedied—who are still "of the Church," if we may quote St Basil himself; and from "parasynagogues." As an example of "heretic" St Basil gives the Montanists, who "baptize into names that have not been handed down to us" and therefore are not baptized at all. These and others of their kind the Apostolic Canon, St Basil and the fathers called "heretics." They are heretics properly so-called; others are called "heretics" by extension.[8]

Similar explanations can be found in the standard commentators. Balsamon pointed out the necessity of distinguishing how the terms "heretic" and "schismatic" are used in different contexts;[9] and both he and Zonaras call attention to the role of correct form as a criterion for true baptism.[10] At the same time, abuses arising from an exaggerated reliance on form were avoided. Manifestly falsified content invalidated baptism even if the proper form was employed. Thus certain Saracens who had themselves and their children baptized in the belief that this conferred invulnerability were to be regarded as unbaptized.[11] Intention, in other words, is to be taken into consideration as well as form.

But what of Cyprian? The standard answer in Byzantium would relegate him and his position to the dustbin of history. St Basil had already regarded Cyprian's baptismal practice as obsolete. He observes (canon 1) that Cyprian and Firmilian had rejected Novatianist baptism, which according to his own system of classification would be accepted, and he briefly summarizes the theological reasoning behind their position. "But since on the whole it has seemed best to some of those in Asia that their [i.e, Novatianist] baptism be accepted *oikonomias heneka tôn pollôn,* let it be accepted." What is meant by the phrase in question? Probably just "for the sake of the discipline (or practice) of the majority."[12] Cyprian's practice had been superseded by that of the many others who, like St Basil himself, argued that the acceptance or rejection of a particular baptism should be based on a theological evaluation of the baptismal form employed. To be sure, the text of Cyprian's baptismal council circulated in eastern canonical collections from antiquity onward; but in the Byzantine period it was frequently abridged and abbreviated, and commentators tended to regard its provisions as obsolete. "This synod is the most ancient of all," write Balsamon and Zonaras; it has considerable historical interest; but it was exclusively an African affair, not universally accepted, and more recent canons have taught us to distinguish in our ways of receiving those who turn from heresy.[13]

I have reviewed the *oikonomia* of baptism at this point because in Byzantium, as in the West, the problems of orders was closely related to that of baptism. With orders as with baptism the question facing the bishop was one of reception: in a given case are clergy coming to the Church from schism or heresy to be received in their orders? Here as with baptism it was necessary to "observe custom and to follow the fathers who have managed church affairs before us."[14] For that very reason, here as with baptism it was necessary to distinguish between the various forms which separation from the Church can take.

The clergy of some groups, like the Paulicians, were to be reordained, should they be deemed worthy, in line with I Nicea's treatment of the followers of Paul of Samosata. "The former ordination, which they received while they were heretics, cannot be considered an ordination," wrote Zonaras, "for how could someone baptized contrary to the Orthodox faith have received the Holy Spirit in the imposition of hands." Therefore when the canon speaks of their deposition (*kathairesis*) should they be found unworthy, it misuses the term, for one can be deposed only if one is truly ordained.[15] On the other hand, under certain conditions the clergy of other groups could be received in their orders, without reordination, in accordance with what was understood to be I Nicea's provisions for the Novatianists and Meletians. Here too the question of orders is closely linked to that of baptism. The ordination of the Paulianists and other heretics properly so called is to be *rejected* along with their baptism. It does not necessarily follow that the ordination of schismatics and those called heretics by extension is to be *accepted* along with their baptism, but in fact the connection was often made, at least during the period in which the Eastern understanding of orders was being formed. In the trinitarian and christological controversies, those demanding reordination of their theological opponents invariably met with this response: if you reordain, logically you must also rebaptize—something which hitherto has never been done. As the fathers' treatment of the various heresies indicates, one reordains only those whom one rebaptizes.[16]

But does not acceptance of the heretics' sacraments in effect create a church outside the Church? Some, worthy heirs to Cyprian, argued precisely that. "Si habent licentiam baptizandi, habent et sacerdotes ordinandi," writes a late Arian bishop to justify his group's move from a policy simply of reordination to one of rebaptism as well: "If they have the capacity to baptize, they also have the capacity to ordain."[17] Severus of Antioch presents an alternative approach to the problem: By denying the true faith, heretics are deprived of every spiritual gift. Their ministrations are without exception infirm, without effect, null. But by the judgment of the bishops, heirs to the powers conferred by Christ on the apostles, the repentant heretic can be received into the true Church, which, far more than God's people of old, is filled with the gifts of the Spirit. Whoever is received into its bosom is completely penetrated by these gifts, just as

Saul's envoys were filled with the Spirit simply by joining with the company of the prophet Samuel.[18]

At this point Severus is simply the most articulate exponent of an understanding of sacramental *oikonomia* common to the eastern churches. In canonical and related literature the sacraments and other ministrations of heretics are never described in very flattering terms. Adjectives like *akuros* (of no force, *irrita*) and *abebaios* (infirm, "shaky") regularly are used to describe them. Worse, they are distinctly harmful. The heretics' eucharist is "real poison";[19] their ordinations are "the tokens of satanic apostasy."[20] Examples could be multiplied. But we should not be misled by a terminology differing from that of a later age. An ordination performed by a bishop invading another's diocese was also *akuros kai abebaios* (Sardica canon 15); an absolute ordination, according to the Council of Chalcedon (canon 6), was *akuros*, the meaning of *akuros* here being clarified by the words that follow: the one thus ordained *mêdamou dunasthai energein*, he cannot serve.[21] The heretics' sacraments are ineffectual, but they are not necessarily non-existent, *nichtig*, invalid in an absolute sense, as the secondary literature so often has supposed. In certain circumstances they could be ratified, confirmed, just as various other ministrations that we today would call irregular were. Needed was not reiteration of the sacrament in question but rather reconciliation: usually anointing with chrism in the case of baptism and blessing by imposition of hands in the case of ordination.[23]

The practice of the fathers indicated that schismatics and heretics *could* be received in their orders. Long catalogs of appropriate precedents, assembled whenever the need arose, demonstrated that clearly. However the very context in which the problem of orders was posed in Byzantium demanded simultaneous investigation of another question: *should* heretics be received in their orders in the case at hand? On this question too the fathers were consulted, but here they provided no pat answers. At II Nicea Patriarch Tarasius might claim that "the fathers are always in harmony with each other" on this subject, that "in them there is no contradiction,"[24] but the context of his remarks—the council's lengthy debate on the reception of repentant iconoclasts—shows how difficult it sometimes was to perceive that harmony. The line between economy and apostasy was not sharply drawn.

Systematic exploration of the application and limits of *oikonomia*—the weighing of the patristic and historical evidence, as it were—began in the wake of the christological controversies and continued through the following centuries. When a new case arose, precedents would be assembled and examined with regard both to their applicability and to their authority. Particularly noteworthy new cases in turn would set the pattern for subsequent ones. In the process certain rules governing *oikonomia* developed.

Of decisive importance in this long history was II Nicea. How were the repentant iconoclast bishops to be received? Patriarch Tarasius presented an impressive dossier of texts in support of reception in orders, but the monastic party—under the leadership of Theodore the Studite's uncle Plato—insisted upon reading into the record another, less generous text: Athanasius' Letter to Rufinian, according to which those constrained by circumstances may be received in their orders, but the "leaders and begetters" of the heresy may not. The iconoclast bishops were acquitted nonetheless. We were born into the heresy, deceived by false teachers, trapped in a common error, they argued plausibly.[25] But a basic principle had been laid down for subsequent cases involving *oikonomia*: if willful, conscious adherence to heresy can be demonstrated, the offender can hope at best for reception as a layman. Needless to say, a great deal thus depends upon what qualifies as heresy. Was the priest who blessed Constantine VI's adulterous second marriage guilty of a disciplinary offense, as those supporting his rehabilitation argued, or of the "moechian heresy," as Theodore the Studite charged? The question was not merely academic.[26]

A further limitation to *oikonomia* developed in the wake of II Nicea. From the time of the council onward, the profession of faith required of a bishop at his ordination incorporated anathemas against those rejecting the council's dogma. Those turning to iconoclasm after its recrudescence in 815 thus stood self-condemned. They had defiled the cross itself, whose sign preceded their signatures. The excuse of ignorance offered by an earlier generation of iconoclasts could no longer be used to justify reception in orders. What had once been an altogether fitting economy is such no longer.[27] The application of "economy" thus comes to be limited by perjury, by failure to uphold not only dogma but also canons and other disciplinary norms spelled out in the bishops' oath, the *Synodikon of*

Orthodoxy, and other formal professions. When, for example, the fabricator of the anti-Photian dossier calls "stauropats" those who rallied to Patriarch Photius after earlier subscribing to his deposition, he is not just trying to be insulting. He is urging their deposition without possibility of restoration.[28]

One more limitation to *oikonomia* must be mentioned. Those not truly ordained, but merely feigning ordination or having a counterfeit ordination may not be received in clerical orders. This may seem obvious, but the texts in which Byzantine canonists see this principle in operation are not so obvious: I Constantinople canon 4 (the case of Maximus the Cynic) and Sardica canons 18-19 (Greek numbering; the case of Museus and Eutychianus). These days the ordination of Maximus the Cynic generally would be regarded as gravely illicit but still valid; however the canon dealing with his case is quite emphatic: "Maximus never was and is not now a bishop; those who have been ordained by him are in no order whatever of the clergy." Clearly this was not just a routine condemnation of an irregular ordination, and in Byzantium at least, the canon was taken literally: Maximus was never a bishop. Few reasons are given for this absolute nullity, but the suggestion is that the blatant illegality of the ceremony performed upon him made it no ordination.[29]

In the *Nomocanon in Fourteen Titles,* and consequently in glosses and commentaries, the case of Maximus the Cynic was linked with that of Museus and Eutychianus. The circumstances of this case are not altogether clear even today.[30] The text itself says that Museus and Eutychianus are not to be accounted bishops and that they are eligible only for the communion of laymen, but it also seems to suggest that clerics ordained by them may be received in their orders. In Byzantium, however, the text was understood in quite a different way. According to Balsamon:

> Museus and Eutychianus, though unordained [*akheirotonetoi*] nonetheless ordained certain clerics as though they were bishops. When therefore Gaudentius [the bishop speaking in canon 18] asked that those ordained by them be received for the sake of peace ... another bishop, named Hosius [of Cordoba; the speaker in canon 19] replied: "Since we are obliged to be fair-minded and philanthropic, we receive into the clergy those who have been ordained by men who are bishops in truth ... Those, however, who were made clerics by Museus and Eutychianus we will admit only to the communion of laymen, because those who ordained

them had no right to bear the name of bishop." Therefore note that there is nothing in the present canon prejudicial to those who were made clerics by the deposed or the anathematized. What is said about Museus and Eutychianus should be understood as referring to those who were not ordained but rather counterfeited ordination [*plasamenous kheirotonian*].[31]

Here again the difference in form between real ordination and counterfeit ordination is not clearly spelled out, but the difference in consequences is: an ordination likened to that of Museus and Eutychianus, or to that of Maximus the Cynic, is to be considered "absolutely null and utterly void."

This principle can be seen in operation particularly clearly in the course of the proceedings against Photius. In the council of 869-70 the bishops ordained by Photius in vain argued that their case was like that of bishops ordained by Acacius or Peter Mongus in the days of the christological controversies. Photius' inveterate opponent Metrophanes of Smyrna had another comparison in mind:

> To say that Peter Mongus of Alexandria was deposed, and likewise Acacius of Constantinople, but that those ordained by them were not, does not justify you or Photius, for the ecclesiastical laws judge bishops who return from heresies differently from those elevated by adulterers and contrary to the canon ... They in no way receive those consecrated as you and Photius were, in line with what the holy and universal second council [I Constantinople] determined concerning Maximus the Cynic and those ordained by him.[32]

Metrophanes' point carried the day. The council's fourth canon closely follows the wording of I Constantinople canon 4: Photius "never was and is not now a bishop," and those ordained by him are not to remain in whatever orders they thus received.[33] This canon, however, proved not only unpopular but also unworkable. Photius, of course, was restored to the patriarchate; those ordained by him in time came to include even a younger son of the emperor. Eventually even Stylianus of Neocaesarea, an old-guard anti-Photian, is moved to suggest what he believes would be an appropriate compromise. Writing to Pope Stephen V he quietly drops the example of Maximus the Cynic and instead invokes the principle laid down at II Nicea: "The heads of heresies and schisms are to be cast out, but the rest can be received by economy."[34] Photius may still be a heresiarch, but at least he is acknowledged as ordained; while he cannot be received in his orders, those ordained by him may be.

This examination of *oikonomia*, its powers and its limitations, could continue. Additional cases could be cited, further developments could be noted, other aspects could be explored. But even this survey suggests the need for greater precision in the use of this term. In Byzantium at least, *oikonomia* was not understood as a limitless power to make what otherwise is invalid to be valid should that be expedient, as so many modern presentations have claimed. Rather, *oikonomia* was seen above all as prudent pastoral administration of the basis of the canons and the example of the fathers. By definition it was expected to operate within certain universally recognized limits and according to certain well-defined patterns.

This examination of *oikonomia* also suggests the need for greater caution when speaking of differences between eastern and western approaches to orders. There are differences, to be sure, particularly from the twelfth century onward. In the West distinctions between the power of orders and the power of jurisdiction, between validity and liceity or fruitfulness, certainly were suggested in the works of Augustine and the fathers and implicit in the practice of the Church, but they were systematically developed and explored in the nascent schools. In Byzantium, on the other hand, orders and their "economy" remained the domain of bishops and their chanceries. The courtroom, not the classroom, set the tone. Distinctions developed from case to actual case, not from *causa* to hypothetical *causa.* Yet these differences in context do not necessarily mean fundamental differences in ecclesiology and sacramental theology. Byzantine canonists and churchmen had little opportunity or incentive to examine questions of validity apart from those of lawful exercise or fruitfulness, but when the need arose they did in fact distinguish the non-existent from the merely defective. When a case demanding "economy" arose, the Byzantine bishop was guided by principles closer to those of Augustine than to those of Cyprian.

The examples from antiquity and the Byzantine Middle Ages which I have reviewed in this essay by no means provide a comprehensive sacramental theology, but they do suggest some general principles which should be kept in mind when the question of reception of non-Orthodox clergy into the Orthodox Church is discussed today:

1. The Orthodox Church accepts that which it can recognize *as its own*, that which is "of the Church." In determining this, clear and objective criteria must be employed. Thus, the Church rejects the baptism of those groups which have established their own baptism as distinct from the Church's—Montanist baptism "in the name of the Father and of the Son and of the Lord Montanus," for example. So also the Church rejects the counterfeit ordination of persons like Museus and Eutychianus. But if the Church's baptism or ordination is in fact present, it is to be accepted as such, even when external pressures or deep-seated antipathies might tempt us to reiteration. Here, in other words, I would take exception to the practice and theory of rebaptism and reordination which has developed in some Orthodox churches since the eighteenth century. Certainly for the Church in antiquity and throughout the Byzantine Middle Ages, it was heresy "properly so-called," deliberately expressed in word, gesture and matter, that nullified, and not simply the fact of separation, schism, as Cyprian claimed.

2. We must also remember that in Byzantium a distinction in practice was drawn between ordination itself and its fruitfulness and lawful exercise, as the many debates over reception of heretics indicate. This has obvious implications for reception of non-Orthodox clergy into the Orthodox Church today. To say that we can in general accept the ordination of non-Chalcedonians, for example, does not mean that in each and every case we should and must admit them to exercise of a clerical ministry in our Church. A bigamous priest coming from outside the canonical limits of Orthodoxy should not be accepted to priestly ministry any more than a bigamous priest ordained within the Orthodox Church should be permitted to continue to exercise priestly ministry. Bigamy—clearly condemned not only by Apostolic Canon 17 but also in 1 Tim 3:2, "a bishop must be the husband of *one wife*"—disqualifies both of them for such service, but this does not mean that either of them should be regarded as though never ordained.

3. But what precisely is meant by "ordination?" How is "real" ordination or "real" baptism to be distinguished from the "counterfeit"? On this point Byzantine sources offer no pat answer. On the one hand, they draw

attention to the role of correct form. This is particularly true in the case of baptism, but the same concern can be seen in the case of orders. For example, Museus and Eutychianus are specifically described as "unordained." At the same time, these sources do not regard correct form as sufficient in itself, without reference to the faith and life of the Church, as the example of the Saracens "baptized" in expectation of gaining invulnerability indicates. They never speak of the sacraments without some reference to ecclesial context—a point generally neglected by Moghila, his sources and his heirs, but accentuated and indeed exaggerated by proponents of the economic approach to sacramental theology. This emphasis on ecclesial context accounts for the Byzantine canonists' emphatic rejection of the notion of "absolute ordination." For them, as for Orthodoxy today, the charism received in ordination is not regarded as an isolated objective grace ontologically possessed by an individual who stands somehow outside or above the Church. Rather, it is relational; like all the other gifts in the Church it is exercised with and for the others.[35]

4. This affirmation has dramatic implications for ecclesiology. If "validity" (or "authenticity," to use a word with fewer associations) cannot be evaluated apart from ecclesial context, apart from the community of faith, what does this say about groups separated from the Orthodox Church? The Orthodox have not clearly responded to this question, but some response is desperately needed. There is sometimes a tendency in our modern Orthodox ecclesiology to identify the limits of the Church purely and simply with limits of canonical Orthodoxy, so that if we apply the word "church," e.g., to the Roman Catholic Church or the Coptic Church, we do so simply by convention or courtesy, without in fact assigning churchly quality to these bodies any more than we do to the Mormons' "Church of Jesus Christ of Latter Day Saints." In short, even when we do not explicitly invoke "the Orthodox principle of economy," we invoke one of its basic principles: outside the Orthodox Church as we see it there is simply undifferentiated darkness in which the Pope is no different than a witchdoctor. While we may sometimes be willing to speak of separated *Christians,* i.e., isolated individuals who at some point or another have received a "valid" trinitarian baptism, we are reluctant to speak of separated *churches.* Orthodox churchmen in other centuries have been less diffident. Here we may note particularly St Basil the Great.

Certainly he, if anyone, refused to identify completely the charismatic and the canonical limits of the Church.

5. A final point should also be mentioned. The charge is sometimes made that, if we recognize the "validity" or "authenticity" of sacraments administered outside the canonical limits of the Orthodox Church, we are as it were condoning the establishment of an anti-Church bent on our destruction. If the sacraments of the separated churches were indeed *theirs* there might be some force to this argument. But are the sacraments administered by the non-Chalcedonians and the Roman Catholics—and maybe by others as well—truly non-Chalcedonian or Roman Catholic sacraments as distinct from the Church's sacraments, in the way, e.g., that Montanist baptism is distinct from the Church's baptism? Certainly not. These sacraments—which are in fact the Church's sacraments—point beyond division, schisms and even false teaching to that fulness of unity in truth and love which is proper to Orthodoxy, so that when, e.g., a Roman Catholic is baptized, he becomes a member of the body of Christ, not a servitor of the Pope; and when he is ordained, it is for the upbuilding of that body, not for promotion of the *filioque*. To be sure, schism and false teaching ("heresy by extension," as St Theodore of Studios would call it) may hinder or prevent these sacraments from fully achieving their right end, but they do not make them non-existent or deprive them of all meaning and content. In and through them the work of God's Church—our Church—continues. In this, at least, we should rejoice, even if we must also lament the realities of schism and heresy.[36]

NOTES

1 Further discussion: J. Erickson, "*Oikonomia* in Byzantine Canon Law," in *Law, Church, and Society: Essays in Honor of Stephan Kuttner*, ed K. Pennington and R. Somerville (Philadelphia 1977) 225-36, and "Reception of Non-Orthodox into the Orthodox Church," *Diakonia* 19 (1984/85) 68. Convenient bibliography: Y. Congar, "Propos en vue d'une théologie de l'Économie' dans le la tradition latine," *Irenikon* 45 (1972) 155-206 at p 179 n 2. For a survey of positions and critical analysis: F. J. Thomson, "Economy," *Journal of Theological Studies* n.s. 16 (1965) 368-420. More recent: P. Raï, "L'Économie dans droit canonique byzantin des origines jusqu'au XIe siècle," and "L'Économie chez les

Orthodoxes depuis 1755," and K. Duchatelez, "Le principe de l'économie baptismale dans l'antiquité chrétienne," all in *Istina* 18 (1973) 260-368.

2   Congar, "Propos ...," K. McDonnell, "Ways of Validating Ministry," *Journal of Ecumenical Studies* 7 (1970) 209-65; L. M. Knox, *The Ecclesial Dimension of Valid Orders* (Catholic University Canon Law Studies 477, Washington, DC 1971). Exploration of the ecumenical implications of "economy" was initiated by Anglicans concerned about the validity of their orders, above all by J. A. Douglas, *The Relations of the Anglican Churches with the Eastern Orthodox* (London 1921), "The Orthodox Principle of Economy," *The Christian East* 13 (1939) 99-109, and elsewhere.

3   See Erickson, "*Oikonomia ...*" and "Penitential Discipline in the Orthodox Canonical Tradition," chapter 2 above.

4   Cf. the *entalma* for a spiritual father, PG 119, cols 1152-3.

5   Synod in Trullo canon 102.

6   The *Epistola Ecclesiae Constantinopolitanae ad Martyrium Antiochenum episcopum* (ed J. -B. Pitra, *Juris ecclesiastici Graecorum historia et monumenta* 1 [Rome 1864] 187-8), which in a slightly abbreviated form circulated as I Constantinople canon 7; Timothy of Constantinople, *De receptione haereticorum* (PG 86, cols 9-74, better ed: V. Benesehvich, *Drevne-slavianskaia Kormchaia XIV Titulov bez tolkovanii* 1 [St Petersburg 1906] 707-38); office for the reception of heretics in the Barberini *Euchologion* (ed J. Goar, *Euchologion siue Rituale Graecorum* [Venice 1730, repr Graz 1960] 694-5); Synod in Trullo canon 95.

7   *Ep.* II, 63, PG 99, col 1281C: *Egô de Kuprianizein ... ôêthên.*

8   *Ep.* I, 40, PG 99, cols 1052D-1053B, referring to Basil the Great canon 1.

9   Commentary on I Constantinople canon 6, PG 137, col 337A.

10 Commentaries on Apostolic Canons 47 and 49, PG 137 cols 132B-33B, 137AB.

11 G. Ficker, "Erlasse des Patriarchen von Konstantinopel Alexios Studites," *Festschrift der Universität Kiel zur Feier des Geburtsfestes Seiner Majestäts des Kaisers und Königs Wilhelm II* (Kiel 1911) 14.

12 Thus R. Deferrari in his translation of Basil's *Letters* 3 (Loeb Classical Library, Cambridge, MA and London 1962) 17. Such translations as "pour le bien d'un grand nombre" (P. Joannou, *Discipline générale antique* [Pont. Com. per la Redazione del Cod. Dir. Can. Orientale, *Fonti*, fasc. 9, Grottaferrata 1963] vol 2, 97) or "par motif de condescendance pour beaucoup" (P. Dumont, "Economie ecclésiastique et réitération des sacrements," *Irenikon* 14 [1937] 228-47, 339-62, at p 236) are sheer eisegesis.

13 PG 137, cols 1096-7, 1104.

14 Basil the Great canon 1.

15 Commentary on I Nicea canon 19, PG 137, col 305CD. On the identification of the medieval Paulicians with the ancient Paulianists cf. Balsamon, commentary on I Nicea canon 19, PG 137, cols 301D-5B.

16 Thus Severus, ed E. W. Brooks, *The Sixth Book of the Select Letters of Severus, Patriarch of Antioch* 2 (trans Oxford 1904) 180-1, 184. Cf. the case of the sixth-century bishop Paul of Aphrodisias, whose reordination at the hands of the Chalcedonians led his former clergy to label him "the rebaptized." Recounted in L. Saltet, *Les Réordinations* (Paris 1907) 54-5.

17 Maximinus, in F. Kauffmann, *Aus der Schule des Wulfila* Auxentii Dorostorensis epistula de fide vita et obitu Wulfilae *im Zusammenhang der* Dissertatio Maximini contra Ambrosium (Strassburg 1899) 78; quoted by Saltet, 48.

18 Brooks, *The Sixth Book*, 183-4, 353-4. C. H. Turner very rightly notes the similarities between Severus and Augustine at this point in his "Apostolic Succession," in *Essays on the Early History of the Church and the Ministry*, ed H. B. Swete (2nd ed Macmillan, London 1921) 95-214 at pp 211-4.

19 Theodore of Studios, *Ep.* II.24, PG 99, col 1189. This and additional examples from Theodore in J. Hergenröther, "Die Reordinationen der alten Kirche," excursus to his *Photius: Patriarch von Konstantinopel* 2 (Regensburg 1867, repr Darmstadt 1966) 321-76 at pp 340-1.

20 G. Ficker, "Erlasse ..." 14.

21 Additional examples and analysis in Hergenröther, 325-6.

22 This is surely the sense of *Questiones et responsiones ad orthodoxos* 14, PG 6, col 126D: *Tou hairetikou epi tên orthodoksian erkhomenou to sphalma diorhountai, tês men kakodoksias tê metathesei tou phronêmatos, tou de baptismatos tê epikhrisei tou hagiou murou, tês de kheirotonias tê kheirothesia,* "The fault of the heretic coming to right belief is to be set right thusly: that of bad belief by change of thinking, that of baptism by anointing with the holy myron, and that of ordination by the imposition of hands."

24 J. D. Mansi, *Sacrorum Conciliorum Nova et Amplissima Collectio*—cited hereafter in this essay as Mansi—vol 12, col 1050C.

25 Mansi 12, col 1031D.

26 Further discussion: Erickson, *"Oikonomia ..."* 233 and n 43.

27 Nicephorus of Constantinople, *Apologeticus Minor* 6, PG 100, cols 840D-1C.

28 Mansi 16, cols 441-3.

29 Cf. Balsamon and Zonaras, PG 137, cols 328-9.

30 H. Hess, *The Canons of the Council of Sardica* (Oxford 1958) 56, 68; J. Hefele, *Histoire des conciles* 1.2 (ed H. Leclercq, Paris 1907) 801-2.

31 PG 137, cols 1485D-7B.

32 Mansi 16:91DE.

33 Mansi 16:162AB, 400E.

34 Mansis 16:439A.

35 Cf. the remarkable essay of J. Zizioulas, "Ordination and Communion," *Study Encounter* vol 6, no 4 (WCC, Geneva 1980) 187-92, especially 189-90, now included in his *Being as Communion* (St Vladimir's Seminary Press, Crestwood, NY 1985) 209-46.

36 Cf. G. Florovsky's very favorable assessment of Augustine's understanding of the sacraments, in "The Limits of the Church," *Church Quarterly Review* 11 (Oct. 1933) 117-31 at 128: "... the love of God overlaps and surmounts the failure of love in man. In the sects themselves and even among heretics the church continues to perform her saving and sanctifying work. It may not follow, perhaps, that we should say, the schismatics are *still in the church*; at all events this would not be very precise and sounds equivocal. It would be truer to say, the church continues to work in the schisms in expectation of the mysterious hour when the stubborn heart will be melted in the warmth of 'preparatory grace,' when will burst into flame and burn the will and thirst for unity and communality. The 'validity' of the sacraments among schismatics is the mysterious guarantee of their return to Catholic plenitude and unity."

Chapter 9

Leavened and Unleavened:
Some Theological Implications of the
Schism of 1054*

As one of the most dramatic and portentous events of the Middle Ages, the schism of 1054 has merited meticulous scholarly treatment.[1] But while its outlines are well known, interpretations of the schism have varied. The traditional assessment would see the events of 1054 as marking a definitive break or rupture, caused by the ambitions of the Reform Papacy or by the natural rebelliousness of the Byzantine Church, depending on one's point of view.[2] Recent scholarship, on the other hand, has tended to minimize the importance of 1054, with one school of interpretation arguing that the real schism of East and West had occurred long before,[3] and another school emphasizing the fact that Byzantium and Rome continued to enjoy friendly ecclesiastical relations well beyond 1054.[4]

All these interpretations share at least one characteristic: a tendency to neglect or underestimate the religious questions raised in 1054. This is not too surprising, given the nature of these questions. The Greek polemicists of the day castigated the Latins for their dietary habits, for failing to sing "Alleluia" during Lent, for fasting on Saturdays, but above all for their use of unleavened bread—azymes—in the eucharist. In response,

---

* Originally published in *St. Vladimir's Theological Quarterly* 14 (1970) 3-24. I have not attempted to revise this early essay to take into account more recent literature, above all the major study of H. Mahlon Smith, *And Taking Bread ...: Cerularius and the Azyme Controversy of 1054* (=Théologie Historique 47, Éditions Beauchesne, Paris 1978). That work, apparently written with no acquaintance with my own essay, presents a detailed account of the controversy of 1054 and analyzes the relationship of the principle documents pertaining to it, though without going beyond printed sources to manuscripts such as those mentioned below, n 33. My own assessment of the "theological implications" of the controversy therefore may remain of some interest to students of Eastern Christian thought and to ecumenists.

the Latins extended the debate to such problems as clerical celibacy and the wearing of beards by the clergy.

From at least the time of Baronius, historians have regarded all these issues simply as pretexts, devoid of religious significance, cunningly seized upon by Michael Cerularius to arouse the emotions of the masses and to further his own ambitious schemes.[5] Modern dogmaticians of both East and West, tacitly assenting to this judgment, have directed attention instead to the questions of papal primacy and *filioque*.[6] Yet in 1054 and for several decades thereafter, neither of these issues was given much emphasis, at least by the Byzantines. Papal primacy (or rather preeminence) is never directly attacked. Even Michael Cerularius refers to the pope with the greatest respect and prefers to cast the blame for the whole affair on his old enemy Argyrus, the Byzantine military governor in southern Italy, or else on the "Franks."[7] Though Cardinal Humbert perhaps pushes the claims of the see of Peter beyond the limits set by previous generations, the East seems not to have noticed. Peter of Antioch, for example, can still expound the theory of the pentarchy as though the position of the papacy had not changed since the eighth century.[8] Likewise the *filioque* problem, so prominent in the ninth century, receives comparatively little attention in eleventh-century anti-Latin polemics. To be sure, in 1053 there was a disputation on the subject between the Greeks and Latins at Bari, for which the pope prepared a list of prooftexts from Paul and upon which Humbert probably based his *Rationes de sancti spiritus processione a patre et filio*.[9] But the Constantinopolitans themselves at first ignored the issue. Only after Cardinal Humbert castigated the Greeks for *dropping filioque* from the creed did they resurrect the appropriate works of Photius;[10] and even then it was only Theophylact of Bulgaria who chose to *center* his attention on the problem.[11] As the amount of ink and parchment expended would indicate, for most Byzantine churchmen of the eleventh and twelfth centuries the principal point of disagreement with the Latins was not papal primacy or *filioque* but rather the use of unleavened bread in the eucharist. As one patriarch of Antioch writes: "The chief and primary cause of division between them and us is in the matter of azymes ...The matter of azymes involves in summary form the whole question of true piety."[12]

Those of humbler station, both Latins and Greeks, seem to have shared this judgment. As modern historians have pointed out, chroniclers of the period mention the schism on 1054 only in passing;[13] but when they do mention the schism, the sole cause given for it is the issue of the bread of the eucharist. The earliest such Byzantine reference remarks simply, "Patriarch Michael Cerularius expunged the Pope from the diptychs on account of the azymes."[14] On the Latin side, Cardinal Humbert's bull excommunicates Cerularius and his followers as "prozymite heretics,"[15] and the *vita* of Leo IX states that in his pontificate arose the "heresy of the leavened-breaders."[16] On a popular level as well, both Latins and Greeks recognized the problem. For example, most contemporary accounts of the crusades recount at least one occasion on which the Greeks purify an altar after a Latin-rite mass has polluted it.[17]

Even if we subscribe to the prevailing opinion—that Michael Cerularius introduced the whole issue to arouse popular support for his own schemes—we must at least acknowledge that the patriarch's choice of an issue touched the spleens of many of his contemporaries. Though today the problem of the bread of the eucharist might seem at most an indifferent question of liturgical custom and of humanly established ecclesiastical discipline, for the medieval Byzantines "the whole question of true piety was involved" and hence no mere human ordinance could license the use of azymes.[18] Two questions arise: Why was the problem of azymes once such a lively theological issue? Why is that issue now so dead?

Consubstantial and supersubstantial

Today our natural tendency in investigating a problem like that of the eucharistic bread might be to search out the origins of the use of azymes in the eucharist.[19] However, Byzantine polemicists of the eleventh and twelfth centuries show no such tendency. Most of their arguments against unleavened bread draw rather from those two great medieval arsenals, etymology and symbolism.

The general pattern of the etymological arguments can be set forth succinctly: "According to all the Gospel accounts of the Last Supper, Jesus took *artos*. But *artos* is derived from *airô* and *epairô* and *pherô epi ta anô*—to elevate and raise up and carry to the heights." Therefore the

bread employed must have been leavened.[20] Now modern lexicons know
no such etymology. However, a late tenth-century Byzantine lexicon gives
a very similar derivation: *ek tou airô tou sêmainontos to pherô.*[21]

Other arguments, derived from philology rather than from etymology,
also occur constantly: "In Scripture the word *artos,* when used without a
modifier like *azumos,* always refers to perfect leavened bread, just as the
word *anthropos,* when used without a modifier like *thnêtos,* always refers
to a living man";[22] and "The fathers often use *ta azuma* as a substantive in
explicit contrast to *artos.*"[23] While all these arguments obviously made
little impact on the Latins, to Byzantine Greeks they must have appeared
conclusive.

More involved, but also more suggestive, are arguments which for lack
of a better word may be called symbolic. Now the Latins, when they
bothered at all with such arguments, claimed that their use of azymes was
justified on the grounds that Christ's incarnation was free from the
corruption of original sin, i.e., from the leaven of malice and wickedness.[24] And as proof for their equation of leaven with sin they cited Mt
16:6, "Beware the leaven of the Pharisees and of the Sadducees," and,
more persistently, 1 Cor 5: 6-8:

> Know ye not that a little leaven leaveneth the whole lump? Purge out therefore
> the old leaven, that ye may be a new lump, as ye are unleavened. For even Christ
> our passover is sacrificed for us. Therefore let us keep the feast, not with old
> leaven, neither with the leaven of malice and wickedness; but with the unleav-
> ened (bread) of sincerity and truth.

Here a problem in translation arises. The Greek text reads: "*Ouk oidate
hoti mikra zumê holon to phurama zumoi?*" The Latin text, however,
reads: "Nescitis quia modicum fermentum totam massam *corrumpit?*"
The Latins consequently saw this reference to leaven in a very bad light.
But the Greeks, a bit too ingeniously perhaps, occasionally extract from
this same verse a very opposite meaning: that we should be leavened by
the new leaven which is Christ.[25]

The Greeks too draw some of their symbolic arguments from biblical
texts which happen to mention leaven, e.g., Mt 13:33: "The kingdom of
God is like unto leaven …"[26] However, most of their arguments are
directed to demonstrating the heretical implication of the opponent's
position—the standard procedure in all medieval polemical literature.

Thus, "To employ bread without leaven is to imply that Christ was without a human soul and thus to fall into the heresy of Apollinaris";[27] or, "To employ bread without leaven is to deny that Christ was God as well as man, and thus to fall into the heresy of Nestorius";[28] or, "To employ bread without leaven as a sign of divine purity is to deny the reality of the incarnation, and thus to fall into the heresies of Manes, Valentinus, Apollinaris, Paul of Samosata, Eutyches, Dioscorus, Severus, Sergius, and Pyrrhus."[29]

Such arguments tended to proliferate in the course of debate, tending more toward ingenuity than edification. But one underlying presupposition remains constant: the use of leavened bread in the eucharist is a necessary guarantee for orthodox christology. There were at the time good reasons for this presupposition. Byzantine readers of Epiphanius would have known that in ancient times the Ebionites had combined a woefully inadequate christology with the use of water and unleavened bread in a simulacrum of the eucharist.[30] Closer at hand, still very much alive and active in Asia Minor and Bulgaria, were Paulicians, Bogomils and diverse other Manichean sects, who coupled docetism with a denial of the real presence of Christ in the eucharist, calling the bread of the eucharist the Lord's Prayer and the cup of the eucharist the New Testament.[31] More importantly, the neighboring Armenians were Monophysites and employed unleavened bread in the eucharist as a expression of one divine nature in Christ.[32] Given such groups, the Byzantines not unnaturally viewed Latin use of azymes as an indication of some underlying christological heresy.

This Byzantine concern for the relation between christology and the elements of the eucharist in part explains the frequent use of christological terminology in polemical tracts against the azymites, whether Latin or Armenian. Indeed, these many tracts are a sequel of sorts to the christological debates of the fifth and sixth centuries and the anti-iconoclast literature of the eighth and ninth centuries. The Byzantine position is put most succinctly by Nicetas Stethatus, whose arguments occur both in his 1054 debate with Cardinal Humbert and in his anti-Armenian tracts.[33] He writes:

Those who still partake of the azymes are under the shadow of the law and eat of the table of the Jews, not of the reasonable and living table of God nor of the bread which is both supersubstantial and consubstantial to us men who have believed. For we have been taught to ask for supersubstantial bread from on high. For what is supersubstantial if not that which is consubstantial to us? But the bread which is consubstantial to us is nothing other than the Body of Christ, who was born consubstantial to us according to his humanity. But if our lump's nature (which the Word assumed) is living [or: possesses a soul], you, by partaking of the azymes, do not eat bread which is supersubstantial and consubstantial to us. For indeed the azymes plainly are lifeless [or: without a soul], as the very nature of things even more plainly teaches.[34]

Stethatus' argument is not without certain logical defects: that unleavened bread is any more lifeless than leavened is by no means self-evident.[35] But the thrust of his argument is obvious. That supersubstantial bread which we request in the Lord's Prayer and of which we partake in the eucharist is also consubstantial to us.[36]

Behind Stethatus' argument lies the Greek fathers' emphasis on salvation as deification. "God became man so that man might become divine."[37] But if the whole man is to be divinized, Christ must have been fully consubstantial to man, in body, mind and soul. By extension, Christ in the eucharist must be fully consubstantial to man if the whole man is to participate in his divinity. Stethatus' conclusion—that the bread of the eucharist therefore must be leavened—may seem the product of an overly systematic and literal mind, but his position on the eucharist faithfully reflects the central concern of Byzantine liturgical theology. Stethatus would be in perfect accord with Nicholas Cabasilas' classic statement on the subject:

For [our Lord] not only assumed a body but also soul, mind, will, and all that is appropriate to human nature, in order to be able to unite himself to our whole being ... For as God, he descends to the earth and raises us up from here below. He makes himself man and makes man divine. He who has vanquished sin in one body and one soul frees human nature entirely from blame and releases every man from his sins and unites him to God ... For as it was impossible for us to raise ourselves to him in order to participate in the things which are his, he descended to us to share in the things which are ours. And so precisely does he conform to the things which he assumed that, in giving those things to us which he has received from us, he gives himself to us. Partaking of the body and blood of his humanity, we receive God himself in our souls—the body and blood of God and the soul, mind, and will of God—no less than his humanity.[38]

Stethatus' view of the eucharist—and the theological tradition which produced it—left Cardinal Humbert completely unmoved, and he quickly rejected Stethatus' argument as a piece of futile sophistry:

> As for what you also said—that the consubstantial and the supersubstantial are the same—it is altogether worthless. For although the Lord Jesus is consubstantial to us in humanity, in divinity—in which he is consubstantial to the Father—he us supersubstantial to us. Thus, although the breads of a human table are consubstantial to themselves, the bread of the divine table is supersubstantial to them.[39]

Here, as in his altercation with Berengar, that remarkable eleventh-century Western eucharistic heretic, Humbert wishes to stress the substantial conversion of the elements of the eucharist. For him, a *signum* which was not also *essentialiter res* in no way would be a sacrament.[40] Hence he feels compelled to deny Stethatus' claim that the consecrated elements of the eucharist remain consubstantial to ordinary human breads. Such talk, Humbert would maintain, comes dangerously close to Berengar's contention that the bread of the eucharist is merely a *figura* of the body of Christ. Like an anonymous Roman deacon at the anti-Berengarian Synod of Vercelli (1050), Humbert would ask, "If hitherto we hold only the figure, when will we have the thing itself?"[41]

Humbert need not have been so concerned for Byzantine orthodoxy at this point. More that three hundred years earlier, during the iconoclastic controversy, a position similar to that of Berengar had appeared in Byzantium, and to it St John of Damascus had replied: "The bread and the wine are not merely figures (*antitupa*) of the body and blood of Christ (God forbid!) but the deified body of the Lord itself; for the Lord has said, 'This is my body,' not 'this is a figure of my body' ..."[42] From that time on, the Byzantines seem to have had few doubts concerning the substantial presence of Christ in the eucharist. Thus, in the most important eucharistic controversy to arise in Byzantium itself after iconoclasm, debate concerns not the true presence of the body of Christ but rather the incorruptibility of this body.[43]

Humbert, of course, was not convinced that the Byzantines believed this strongly in the substantial presence of Christ in the eucharist. To him, Stethatus' position—that the eucharist body of Christ remains consubstantial with ordinary bread—implied that in the eucharist there was no ontological change in the elements at all. As for Stethatus' talk of simultaneous consubstantiality and supersubstantiality—utter nonsense! Humbert, like Western theologians from at least the ninth century onward, sees the relation between bread and the body of Christ as the central problem in eucharistic theology. How can mere bread become Christ our Savior? For the Greeks this was not such a great problem, because bread always was considered as at least potentially and metaphorically human flesh. As one Byzantine lexicon states: "Bread signifies both the bread which is eaten and the body."[44] With this understanding of the intimate connection between bread and flesh, St John of Damascus can write:

> Just as in nature the bread by eating and the wine by drinking are changed into the body and blood of the eater and drinker, and do not become a different body from the former one, so the bread of the table and the wine and the water are supernaturally changed by the invocation of the Holy Spirit into the body and blood of Christ, and are not two but one and the same.[45]

In approaching the eucharist the Byzantines began not with bread *qua* bread but with bread *qua* man. Consequently Humbert's central concern—that the substance of lowly bread in some way be effaced and replaced by the body of Christ—remained alien to them. More important was the soteriological question of how man became divine. For Byzantines like Nicetas Stethatus, the answer was clear: by participation in Christ, who in the eucharist as in his earthly life remains both consubstantial and supersubstantial to man.

To be sure, the Latins, unlike the Armenians, maintained the letter of christological orthodoxy; and in charging Humbert with heresy on this point, Stethatus may have been more zealous than wise. Nevertheless, in his approach to the eucharist, Humbert does demonstrate very little awareness of the implications of orthodox christology. Like the Latin tradition generally, Humbert would emphasize the sacrificial rather than the participatory character of the eucharist. Christ, the perfect victim, free from sin (and from leaven), offers himself on Calvary (and in the eucharist) as a sacrifice for sin. There remains little room for the idea of life-giving and deifying participation in a Christ who is at one consubstantial and supersubstantial to us.[46]

Shadow and Reality

A further charge continually leveled by the Greeks against the Latins is one of Judaizing. Leo of Ochrid, whose letter of 1053 sparked the entire controversy, finds the Latins' use of azymes and their practice of fasting on Saturdays above all a reversion to the Jewish law: "For to observe azymes and sabbaths was ordered by Moses. But truly our passover is Christ,"[47] who, in giving to the disciples his blood of the new covenant, clearly wished to show that "those things which were of the old covenant had ceased and passed away."[48] "Moses ordered and legislated that the miserable Jews eat [azymes] once a year with fasting and bitter herbs, saying that they were a symbol of evil passions and tribulation ... But our passover is completely joy and happiness, raising us from earth to heaven through grace..."[49] The observance of azymes and sabbaths, legislated long ago, is abolished and brought to an end through the Gospel. Did not Christ himself heal the paralytic on the sabbath and permit his disciples to pluck grain on the sabbath, thus announcing an end to the servitude of the law?[50] Therefore observation of the Mosaic law and its ordinances should be left to the Jews, who remain under the shadow, ignorant of the light of Christ.[51]

Here, as in the arguments from christology, Byzantine charges are in part the result of the Armenian situation. The Armenians did maintain certain customs which seemed to the Byzantines a little too Old Testamental—restriction of the priesthood to those of priestly descent, for example, and the boiling of joints of meat in the sanctuary for distribution to the priests—and in the largely Greek Synod in Trullo (692) these customs had been explicitly condemned.[52] The Armenian (and Latin) use of unleavened bread in the eucharist appeared to fall in the same category, for the Synod in Trullo also had declared: "Let no man eat the unleavened bread of the Jews, nor have any familiar intercourse with them, nor summon them in illness, nor receive medicines from them."[53]

In addition, Byzantine sensitivity to Judaizing tendencies probably was intensified by Byzantium's long tradition of animosity toward the Jews. In the relatively urban civilization of the Greek East, a substantial Jewish minority made its presence felt both in the market place and in the realm of religious observances. Hence Christian prelates from at least the time of

St John Chrysostom zealously tried to restrain their flocks from Jewish practices.[54] To such prelates, the Jewish practice *par excellence* was the use of unleavened bread. Thus, a tenth-century Byzantine formula for the renunciation of Judaism places the use of azymes second in a long list of practices to be abjured.[55] It is perhaps significant that Nicetas Stethatus— that prominent opponent of both Latins and Armenians—also wrote a tract against the Jews.[56]

However, the charge of Judaizing raised against the Latins suggests a deeper problem, one which cannot be solved simply by referring to the contemporary Armenian and Jewish situation. Christianity always has been faced with the problem of defining its position *vis-à-vis* its Jewish matrix, of determining the relationship between the law and the gospel. The Byzantines were no exception. They took as their starting point certain commonplaces of the Christian tradition—distinctions between shadow and reality, figure and figured, imperfect and perfect—and subjected them to systematic exposition. The moral law, once engraved on tablets of stone, is perfected by the law of love, now engraved on the hearts of Christians. Similarly, circumcision, burnt offerings, and other aspects of the ceremonial law are perfected and replaced by the Christian rites (baptism, the eucharist, etc.) which they foreshadowed.[57] Typical is a statement by Symeon of Thessalonica:

> Therefore it is not good to reject all the precepts given long ago by God; but it is necessary to examine and employ them spiritually and indeed to correct them for the better... For in place of circumcision, baptism and the sanctified life in Christ is given to us; in place of unreasonable sacrifices, a reasonable and living sacrifice unstained with blood, the true body and blood of Christ through the bread and the cup. Honorable and pure marriage is given to us, not polygamy and fornication. Moreover in place of widowhood, virginity is given—higher than marriage and equal in honor to the state of the angels. In the same way temperance in goods is given in place of intemperance; and fasting is given more loftily than in the law, so that we are to abstain from meat in certain days and seasons. Therefore the law by no means is to be neglected or cast off, but rather it is to be employed more loftily, divinely, and spiritually. For those things pertaining to the law were shadows and symbolic figures, but our mysteries are the truth itself ...[58]

The shadows presented in the Old Testament, in the ceremonial as well as in the moral law, are completed and perfected in a most tangible way by the truth which came into the world with Jesus Christ. That perfect, leavened bread therefore must be employed instead of the lifeless azymes of the Old Covenant appears as a necessary and logical conclusion.

Humbert, of course, accepted no such conclusion. Nor did he fully approve of the Byzantine approach to the law, at least as it was employed by Leo of Ochrid. In his initial attack, Leo had not made any explicit distinction between the Old Testament's ceremonial law and its moral law; and Humbert was quick to attack Leo's position as Manichean or Marcionite. With hot indignation he exclaims:

> Look, so that it might be clear to you: you conceived a complaint and brought forth an iniquity; and, lying against the truth itself and against all of divine scripture, you barked that the very Son of God cursed the law and the azymes which it had established. But O holy, good and venerable law, with all your commands and observances! Whoever has cursed, curses, or will curse you and what pertain to you, even if only a single iota, may he be accursed![59]

Here Humbert's accusations in part are the result of his own faulty translation of Leo's letter. Leo had written: *"Ta de azuma oute anamnêsin ekhousi tou kuriou...hôs môsaika nomothetêmena kai dia tês kainês diathêkês... katargêthenta te kai pauthenta."*[60] But in his translation Humbert renders *katargêthenta* (abolished, made of none effect) as though it were *katarêthenta* (cursed, *maladicta*).[61] In addition, Humbert interprets Leo's words as applying to the entire law, not just to *ta azuma*. But other aspects of Humbert's response to Leo reveal not simply problems of translation but also a different approach to the problem of the law. After this initial panegyric on the law, Humbert settles down to what in effect is an exposition of 2 Cor 3:6, "the letter killeth but the Spirit giveth life." The moral commands of the law are good, but their spirit must be fulfilled as well as their letter.[62] Similarly the spirit of the ceremonial law, though not its letter, must be fulfilled.[63] For carnal observances were enjoined by the law in order to inculcate obedience and spiritual cleanliness. But with the coming of Christ, insistence on these external observances has come to an end, and we instead are to fulfill their spiritual meaning.[64] Like Paul, we do not have our own righteousness, "which is of the law, but that which is through the faith of Christ, the righteousness which is of God by faith" (Phil 3:9). Hence we are not to be judged "in meat, or in drink, or in respect of any holyday or of the new moon, or of the sabbath" (Col 2:16).[65] But the Byzantines, with their insistence on leavened bread, their preoccupation with proper sabbath observance, and their condemnation of strangled meats, are guilty of placing the letter above the spirit. With their insistence on carnal observances, it is really the Byzantines who are Judaizing.[66]

Like the Western tradition generally, Humbert would see the difference between the old covenant and the new covenant principally in terms of a distinction between external observances and the internal spirit, the law of works and the law of faith. Now one logical conclusion of this approach, though Humbert does not reach it, is that men of either covenant, through faith in Christ, are capable of fulfilling the spirit if not the letter of the law—though, to be sure, this is much harder for the Old Testament worthies, since their faith is in a Christ yet to come rather than in a Christ who already has revealed himself.[67] A further conclusion—one which Humbert does reach—is that the details of external observance are relatively unimportant. Hence the Byzantines can keep their leavened bread, if only they stop condemning the Latin use of unleavened.[68]

The Byzantines would look askance at both of these conclusions. The external observances of the law are only shadows of the truth. But the truth which they foreshadowed was not a disincarnate spirit, but the incarnate Christ and the equally tangible sacraments and observances which continue his presence within the Church. Thus the righteous of the Old Testament are saved not simply by a pan-covenantal faith in Christ but by the very person of Christ, who harrowed hell to release them from the bonds of death.[69] Similarly, Christians of the new covenant are deified not simply by faith in Christ and in his perfect sacrifice, but by participation in the incarnate Christ through the sacraments. The Byzantines were vividly aware that the reality of the incarnation lay at the heart of the Christian faith, and they were swift to castigate anything—even indifference to liturgical matters—which seemed to question this reality.

Byzantine emphasis on participation in the person of the incarnate Christ is related closely to another question: wherein lies the unity and authority of the Church? For Cardinal Humbert and later generations of western controversialists, the answer was close at hand: in the Pope, the successor of Peter, established by Christ himself as a rock on which the Church is built. Thus in Leo IX's initial response to the Byzantine charges, probably penned by Humbert, there is no attempt to refute the Byzantine arguments directly. Instead, the standard Petrine passages from the New Testament are brought forward and bolstered by a lengthy account of the Donation of Constantine.[70] The East's long history of heresies is recounted and contrasted to Rome's unfailing orthodoxy.[71] After Jesus Christ the apostolic see of Rome is the head of all the churches of God.[72] Consequently Rome must be the measure of orthodoxy and communion with her the test of orthodoxy.[73]

The see of Peter is at once a visible source of authority and a visible sign of unity for the Church. Hence even Humbert can be fairly tolerant of divergent Eastern practices as long as the authority of Rome is not impugned. He even appears to have permitted the omission of *filioque* from the creed if all other circumstances were favorable. At least Patriarch Peter of Antioch's 1052 systatic letter to Rome,[74] which omits *filioque* but in other respects is most deferential, passed through the papal chancery unchallenged. Later generations of Latin controversialists proved equally accommodating, at least when dealing with the Greeks' use of leavened bread and with other such problems of ritual and symbolism. Anselm, for example, gives the standard Latin arguments for why azymes are preferable to leavened bread; but with a good deal of condescension, he grants the licitness of the Greek practice and the symbolism behind it.[75] Typical is the position expressed in a papal letter brought forward at the union negations of Nympheum (1234), in which the Greeks and the Latins are compared to John and Peter in their race to the sepulcher:

> The Greek, running to the faith with the younger disciple, was not ungrateful for the condescension by which God—compassionate toward human nature—willed to be passible. Therefore, electing to remember this daily, the Greek decided to offer the fermented sacrifice. The Latin, however, arrived with Peter, the elder disciple, at the monument of the letter, from which proceeds the spiritual meaning. He entered first and beheld the linen winding sheet placed there, which had wrapped the holy body (which in turn signifies the Church) and also the cloth which had been over the head. Therefore he elected to celebrate the sacrament of the glorified body more wonderfully in the unleavened bread of sincerity.[76]

The Greeks at Nympheum expressed shock at this statement and exclaimed: "From these words it seems to us that the Lord Pope wishes to approve two traditions."[77] For the Byzantines there could be only one tradition if the Church was truly one; and this one tradition was articulated by the Holy Spirit, speaking through the ecumenical councils and the canons approved by these councils, not by the pope. Hence the Byzantines persistently invoke conciliar canons to support their charges against Latin practices. To be sure, not all the canons cited by the Byzantines were really appropriate. The canons of the Synod in Trullo and of Laodicea which condemned receiving unleavened bread from the Jews were not directly applicable to the problem of the bread of the eucharist.[78] But on other problems the Byzantines could construct a good case: for example, the Latin practice of fasting on Saturdays directly contradicts Apostolic Canon 66 and canon 55 of the Synod in Trullo.[79] Unfortunately for the Byzantines, the Latin canonical tradition had incorporated neither of these canons.[80]

Other Latin practices, however, appeared to be contrary to canonical injunctions which both sides had accepted. Latin enforcement of clerical celibacy clearly contradicted the implications of a long series of pronouncements going back to 1 Tim 3:2, "A bishop then must be blameless, the husband of one wife ..."[81] And Latin use of strangled meats contradicted the decree of the apostolic council of Jerusalem reported in Acts 15:29, " ... abstain from meats offered to idols, and from blood, and from things strangled ..."[82] Humbert tried to refute such canonical objections either by verbal manipulations (in the case of clerical celibacy)[83] or by appealing to the spirit in which the canon had been given (in the case of strangled meats).[84] Later generations employed an easier and sounder approach to such canonical problems. Gratian, for example, commenting on the fact that certain canons of Neocaesarea and Ancyra permitted clerical marriage, remarks:

> The position of the synods of Neocaesarea and Ancyra is understood as arising from time and place: from time, because celibacy of the ministers of the altar had not yet been introduced; from place, because both these synods are oriental, and the oriental church does not maintain a general vow of chastity.[85]

Canonical injunctions can vary with time and place. Hence even the canons approved by the ecumenical councils possess no absolute and universal authority. What, presumably, is necessary is reference to the see of Rome, the guarantor of orthodoxy.

The Byzantines possessed a less flexible attitude toward the canons, particularly toward those backed by the authority of an ecumenical council, for they were inspired by the Holy Spirit himself. The letter of the canons might vary from age to age, if properly sanctioned by an ecumenical council at least. But variations from place to place were impossible, though barbarian invasions or other such calamities might make strict application of the canons impossible. If the Church is one, the Byzantines would argue, surely its canons and above all its eucharistic practice should be one.[86]

Such appeals to the canons, presupposing the authority of the ecumenical councils to speak for the universal Church, frequently occur in Byzantine polemical tracts against the Latins. But for the Byzantines, the ecumenical council was less a *principle* than a *sign* of the unity and authority of the Church. The only real source of unity and authority lay in participation in the person of the incarnate Christ, revealed once in history and still present in the eucharist. For the Byzantines, the Church in a very real sense was the body of Christ. The sincerity of Nicetas Stethatus and the other combatants of 1054 might be questioned when they impugn the orthodoxy of the Latins on the basis of 1 Cor 10:17, "For we many are one bread, one body: for we are all partakers of that one bread",[87] but others express the same sentiments more earnestly and plaintively. For many Byzantines the Latins, by maintaining a different eucharist, did not partake of the same body of Christ and hence were not a part of the same Church. Thus the naive but irenic Patriarch Symeon of Jerusalem writes:

> ... from the first the Latins and we were in agreement on the faith in Christ and on all the orthodox dogmas. Therefore it is not right to suppose that we should have disagreed with respect to the most vital part of the faith, the unbloody sacrifice, and that the Latins should have offered azymes but we leavened bread. For according to the words of Paul—"Christ is not divided" (1 Cor 1:13)—there was no disagreement. Away with the idea that the things pertaining to the sacrifice were performed one way by the Latins and another way by us! ... For did not the Romans (i.e., the Byzantines) and the Latins at that time often concelebrate at one altar?[88]

With such intimacy and such agreement in all things concerning the faith, Symeon goes on to argue, any difference of eucharistic bread clearly would have been impossible. But the use of leavened bread clearly is attested by the practice of all the most ancient churches of the East. And to consider the use of azymes or leavened bread a matter of indifference would be to fall into Nestorianism.[89]

For Symeon, as for many Byzantines, the Church is one because its eucharist is one. Though the ecumenical councils and, indeed, the successors of Peter might be a sign of the unity of the Church, the reality of this unity is the undivided eucharistic body of Christ.

The death of the argument

The greatest flaw in the Byzantine argument against azymes was immediately apparent to the Latins. The first round of Byzantine tracts against the Latin usage had neglected the problem of what kind of bread Christ used on the Maundy Thursday when he celebrated the Last Supper with his disciples. Now the synoptic gospel accounts suggest that the meal which Christ ate with his disciples was the passover and that consequently unleavened bread was employed. The Latins immediately pointed out this fact and from then on Byzantine polemicists were forced to address the question. Their positions are numerous and contradictory:

1. Christ, on the established day (14 Nisan), according to the precept of the law (i.e., with azymes) ate a legal passover after which he instituted the new passover of the eucharist in leavened bread.[90]

2. Christ ate the legal passover on the day before the established day (i.e., on 13 Nisan) with unleavened bread, after which he instituted the eucharist with leavened bread.[91]

3. Christ did not eat the legal passover, since according to John, Christ was crucified on 14 Nisan. Rather, before the first day of unleavened bread he instituted the eucharist with leavened bread.[92]

Yet further refinements and new positions developed in the course of centuries of debate.[93] This proliferation of arguments has, of course, been interpreted as a sign of the futility of the Byzantine position on azymes,[94] but the Byzantines viewed matters differently. For them, the question of the bread of the Last Supper was only of tangential importance. Peter of Antioch, for example, adds his historical arguments as little more than an afterthought.[95] Far more serious (and hence more consistent) were the arguments from symbolism. Typical is Euthymius Zigabenus, who argues that even if Christ did celebrate the Last Supper with azymes, he did so out of necessity, knowing that he was about to be betrayed. But the disciples, illumined by the Holy Spirit and freed from the law by Christ's resurrection, rightly adopted the leavened bread of rejoicing.[96]

Just as Byzantine emphasis on the person of the incarnate Christ left the Latins unmoved, so Latin emphasis on what Christ did left the Byzantines unmoved. The Byzantines were less interested in the fact that Christ *instituted* the eucharist than in the fact that Christ *was* the eucharist. However, the Byzantines could not remain permanently oblivious to the demands of the historical. Latin arguments demanded a reply in their own terms. Perhaps the best of the replies elicited is Eustratius Argenti's *Treatise on the Azymes*, from the mid-eighteenth century. Virtually ignoring the symbolic arguments of his predecessors, Argenti works diligently at harmonizing the synoptics to John's account of the Last Supper.[97] In addition, he rejects the earlier Byzantine view that the Latins' use of azymes had been introduced by one Leucius, a disciple of Apollinaris.[98] In its place he constructs a fairly plausible argument that azymes were first used in Rome sometime between the ninth and eleventh centuries.[99]

By modern standards Argenti's conclusions may seem defective, but his methods mark an advance of sorts over his Byzantine predecessors. He at least tries to answer the historical arguments raised by the Latins. But at the same time, Argenti seems to have missed most of the theological issues raised by earlier generations. Latin emphasis on the historical prevails in his writings. While still rejecting the use of azymes, Argenti in effect has capitulated to Humbert. Polemics against the azymites may continue, but the theology of the prozymites has been quietly buried.

*   *   *   *

In recent years the schism of 1054 rarely has been considered the result of genuine theological disagreement. Historians have chosen to emphasize the clash of two most unpleasant personalities, Humbert and Cerularius—and unpleasant they were. It is perhaps significant that neither Roman Catholicism nor Orthodoxy has canonized its respective protagonist. Modern ecumenists, on the other hand, have preferred to see no clash whatsoever, but simply a series of misunderstandings—and misunderstandings there were. The Latins of 1054 demonstrate little knowledge of the Greek language and of the Greek theological tradition, and the Greeks often seem too preoccupied with contemporary Armenian and Jewish polemics to evaluate properly the Latin position.

Nevertheless several more purely theological issues lie hidden in the multitude of polemical tracts which surround the schism of 1054. Byzantine polemicists show an underlying concern for participation in the person of Jesus Christ, God and man, and an awareness of the Church as, in a very literal sense, the body of Christ; and by emphasizing this intimate connection between christology, ecclesiology and the eucharist, the Byzantines differ from their Latin contemporaries. To be sure, most of the differences are implied rather than expressly stated. John of Antioch's judgment—that "the matter of azymes involves in summary form the whole question of true piety"—seems more the result of an immediate reflex action than of lengthy reflection. Like so many of his contemporaries, John of Antioch was deeply attached to the theological realities which he wished to defend, and as a result he often takes as self-evident propositions which his Latin opponents would seriously question. This failure to explore the seemingly self-evident was to prove unfortunate. Later generations of Orthodox controversialists, while rigorously castigating the azymites, at the same time seem to have lost sight of the deeper theological issues which their predecessors had instinctively defended. As so often happens in theological disputation, the letter ultimately has triumphed over the spirit.

NOTES

1 Particularly important are the investigations of Fr Martin Jugie, whose conclusions are set forward in his *Le schisme byzantin* (Paris 1941), and the many books and articles of Anton Michel, the most important of which is *Humbert und Kerullarios* I and II, Quellen und Forschungen der Görresgesellschaft 21 and 23 (Paderborn 1924 and 1930)—hereafter abbreviated as *Humbert und Kerullarios*. A convenient summary of their findings and extensive bibliography is provided by Richard Mayne, "East and West in 1054," *The Cambridge Historical Journal* 2 (1954) 133-48, on whose presentation these introductory pages heavily rely.

2 Thus L. Bréhier, *Le schisme orientale du XIe siècle* (Paris 1899); V. Laurent, "Le schisme de Michel Cérulaire," *Echos d'Orient* 31 (1932) 97-110; A. Fliche, *La Réforme Grégorienne* I (Louvain 1934); W. Norden, *Das Papsttum und Byzanz* (Berlin 1903).

3 Thus Jugie, *Le schisme byzantin*, 334-45 *et passim*; and Michel, "Von Photius zu Kerullarios," *Römische Quartalschrift* 41 (1933) 125-62.

4 Thus W. Holtzman, "Die Unionsverhandlungen zwischen Kaiser Alexios I und Papst Urban II im Jahre 1089," *Byzantinische Zeitschrift* 28 (1928) 38-67; B. Leib, *Rome, Kiev et Byzance à la fin du XIe siècle* (Paris 1924); *et al.*

5 Caesar Baronius, *Annales Ecclesiastici*, ed Antonio Pagi, vol 17 (Lucca 1745) 99, 101. A more recent elaboration of the same theme is presented by Anton Michel, "Schisma und Kaiserhof im Jahre 1054: Michael Psellos," *L'Eglise et les Eglises*, ed O. Rousseau, I (Louvain 1954) 351-440.

6 E.g., J. Karmires, "The Schism of the Roman Church," *Theologia* 21 (1950) 37-67.

7 Michael Cerularius, *Ep. I ad Petrum Antiochenum*, ed Cornelius Will, *Acta et Scripta quae de controversiis ecclesiae graecae et latinae saeculo undecimo composita extant* (Leipzig 1861)—cited hereafter as Will—pp 174-75.

8 Peter of Antioch, *Ep. ad Domenicum Gradensem*, Will, 211f.

9 Humbert, *Rationes*, in *Humbert und Kerullarios* I, 97-111; for the Synod of Bari see especially pp 101, 121. For Leo's work, see *Humbert und Kerullarios* II, 191-4.

10 *Humbert und Kerullarios*, I, 81-2.

11 Theophylact, *Libellus*, Will, 229-53.

12 John IV Oxita, *De azymis* 2, ed B. Leib, "Deux inédits byzantins sur les azymes au début du XIIe siècle," *Orientalia Christiana* 2 (1924) 113, trans Timothy Ware, *Eustratios Argenti: A Study of the Greek Church under Turkish Rule* (Oxford 1964) 113 n 2.

13 See Mayne, 137 n 24.

14 A twelfth-century gloss to Cedrenus' *Compedium historiarum*, cited by Michel, *Humbert und Kerullarios* I, 31.

15 *Excommunicatio*, Will, 154.

16 *Vita Leonis IX*, II, 9, ed J. M. Watterich, *Pontificum Romanorum qui fuerunt inde ab ex. saec. IX usque ad finem saec. XIII Vitae* (Leipzig 1862) I, 161. This *vita*, traditionally ascribed to Wibert of Toul, more recently has been attributed to Humbert; cf. Mayne, 142.

17 E.g., Odo of Deuil, *De profectione Ludovici VII in orientem*, ed V. G. Berry (New York 1948) 54-7.

18 Indicative of the Byzantine attitude is a conversation during the union negotiations at Nympheum (1234): a Greek archbishop declares, "You ask if the body of Christ can be effected in azymes, and we answer that it is impossible." A Latin, desiring to know his position more fully, asks, "As for what you said—that it is impossible—is it *de jure* impossible or absolutely impossible?" And the Greek replies that it is absolutely impossible. In J. D. Mansi, *Sacrorum Conciliorum Nova et Amplissima Collectio*—cited hereafter in this essay as Mansi—vol 23, col 298.

19 Such an approach is followed by J. Parisot, "Azyme," *Dictionnaire de Théologie Catholique* I (Paris 1903) 2653-64, who provides a convenient account of the matter. A more polemical stance is taken by R. M. Wooley, *The Bread of the Eucharist* (London 1913). To summarize: the primitive Church seems to have been indifferent to what bread was employed in the eucharist, but within the Roman Empire at least, the use of leavened bread gradually came to predominate, with even the Armenians employing leavened bread until about the sixth century. The origin of the use of azymes in the West is clouded in obscurity. Cyprian, Ambrose and Gregory the Great *possibly* refer to the use of azymes, but their statements, made only in passing, cannot be construed as definitive proofs. The first incontestable references to the Western use of azymes occur only in Bede, Rabanus Maurus and Paschasius Radbertus. The use of the azymes possibly was due to physical necessity: the usual practice of the time of reserving the consecrated bread in the wine would demand the use of unleavened bread in order to avoid unfortunate chemical reactions. However, Humbert's criticism of the Greek practice of reservation (*Responsio adversus Nicetae Pectorati*, Will, 146) would suggest that in his day reservation of the sacrament was not practiced in Rome. A more likely solution is that azymes were introduced to heighten the air of sanctity surrounding the eucharist and to separate the bread of the eucharist from ordinary breads.

20 Thus Leo of Ochrid, *Ep. ad Ioannem Tranensem*, Will, 57, and virtually all subsequent Byzantine polemicists.

21 *Etymologicum Gudianum* I, ed Aloysius de Stefani (Leipzig 1909) 209. On the *Etymologicum* see K. Krumbacher, *Geschichte der byzantinischen Literatur*, 2nd ed (Munich 1897) 574.

22 Thus Leo of Preslav, *De azymis*, ed A. Pavlov, *Kritischeskie opyti po istorii drevneishei greko-russkoi polemiki protiv Latiniam* (St Petersburg 1878) 120.

23 Euthymius Zigabenus, *Panoplia dogmatica*, PG 130, col 1180. Zigabenus quotes Chrysostom: "There the letter, here the spirit; there the ark of the covenant, here the virgin; there the rod of Aaron, here the cross; there the azymes, here the bread"—a passage frequently employed against the Latins.

24 Thus Humbert, *Dialogus*, Will, 107-108. This too becomes a commonplace in later encounters.

25 Theorianus, *Disputationes cum Armeniorum Catholico*, PG 133, col 259.

26 Leo of Ochrid, *Ep. ad Ioannem Tranensem*, Will, 57.

27 Nicetas Stethatus, *Contra Latinos et Armenios*, ed J. Hergenröther, *Photius, Patriarch von Constantinopel: Sein Leben, seine Schriften und das griechische Schisma* III (Regensburg 1869) 155.

28 Leo of Preslav, *De azymis*, ed Pavlov, 127.

29 John II of Kiev, *Ep. ad Clementem* [anti-] *Papam*, ed Pavlov, 181.

30 Epiphanius, *Panarion*, 30.16, PG 41, col 432.

31 Thus Zigabenus, *Panoplia,* PG 130, col 1314; cf. Martin Jugie, *Theologia dogmatica christianorum orientalium ab Ecclesia catholica dissidentium* III (Paris 1930) 184-5.

32 Zigabenus, *Panoplia,* PG 130, col 1175, reports on the Armenians' eucharistic symbolism. For the origins of Armenian use of azymes see Leib, "Deux inédits …," 143.

33 The chronology of Stethatus' works has yet to be determined. Stethatus' latest editor, J. Darrouzès, suggests that his anti-Armenian works preceded his anti-Latin tracts of 1054: *Nicétas Stéthatos, Opuscules et lettres* (Paris 1961) 11-12. No definitive answer to this problem is possible until a Moscow MS containing four unpublished anti-Armenian tracts of Stethatus is examined closely.

34 *Dialexis et antidialogus,* ed *Humbert und Kerullarios,* II, 322.

35 Stethatus' position probably is based on one of the treatises on the virtues of plants of which the Middle Ages was so fond, but I have been unable to find his source. On the subject see Krumbacher, 632-34.

36 I have rendered Stethatus' *epiousios* as "supersubstantial," for he is clearly referring to the *epiousion arton* of the Lord's Prayer, which the Greek patristic tradition generally interpreted as supersubstantial. Cf. J. Quasten, *Patrology* (Utrecht/Antwerp 1966) III, 409.

37 Athanasius, *On the Incarnation,* ed E. Hardy, *Christology of the Later Fathers* (Philadelphia 1954) 107.

38 Nicholas Cabasilas, *De vita in Christo,* 4, PG 150, col 592.

39 *Responsio,* Will, 137-138. Humbert appears not to have noticed Stethatus' reference to the Lord's Prayer—not unnaturally since the Latin translation reads "panem nostrum *quotidianum* da nobis hodie …"

40 On Humbert's eucharistic thought see Ovidio Capitani, "Studi per Berengario di Tours," *Bolletino dell' Istituto Storico Italiano* 69 (Rome 1957) 154ff.

41 Quoted by A. J. MacDonald, *Berengar and the Reform of Sacramental Doctrine* (London 1930) 81.

42 John of Damascus, *Exposition of the Orthodox Faith,* trans Salmond, A Select Library of Nicene and Post-Nicene Fathers, 2nd ser, vol 9, 83. On the iconoclasts' position toward the eucharist, see Jugie, *Theologia Dogmatica* III, 183.

43 On this debate, initiated by Michael Glykas, see Jugie, *Theologia Dogmatica* III, 321-9, and Hans-Georg Beck, *Kirche und Theologische Literatur im Byzantinischen Reich* (Munich 1959) 654ff.

44 *Etymologicum Gudianum* I, ed Stefani, 209.

45 John of Damascus, *Exposition,* 83.

46 On this distinction in an earlier period cf. Gregory Dix, *The Shape of the Liturgy* (London 1945) 154ff.

47 *Ep. ad Ioannem Tranensem,* Will, 56.

48 Ibid. 57.

49 Ibid. 57.

50 Ibid. 58.

51 Ibid. 60.

52 Synod in Trullo, canons 33 and 99.

53 Ibid. canon 11, trans Percival, A Select Library of Nicene and Post-Nicene Fathers, 2nd ser, vol 14, 370.

54 On Byzantine anti-Jewish literature see Beck, 333ff.

55 F. Cumont, "Une formule grècque de renonciation au judaisme," *Wiener Studien* 24 (1902) 462-72.

56 *Contra Judaeos,* ed Darrouzès, 412-43.

57 A visiting Nestorian physician, Ibn-Butlan, indicates that such views were emphasized in Constantinople in 1054. Georg Graf, "Die Eucharistielehre des Nestorianers Al-Muhtar Ibn Butlan," *Oriens Christianus* 34 (1937) 44-70, 175-91.

58 *Dialogus contra haereses,* PG 155, cols 109-11.

59 *Dialogus,* Will, 110-11.

60 *Ep. ad Ioannem Tranensem,* Will, 58.

61 *Ep. Leonis Achridani ... ab Humberto in Latinum sermonem translata,* Will, 63.

62 *Dialogus,* Will, 115.

63 Ibid. 116.

64 Ibid. 116-7.

65 Ibid. 117.

66 Ibid. 119-20.

67 Cf. Thomas Aquinas, *Summa Theologica* I-II, Q. 103, a. 2, c., trans Fathers of the English Dominican Province, vol 6 (London 1915) 229-30: "However, it was possible at the time of the Law, for the minds of the faithful, to be united by faith to Christ incarnate and crucified; so that they were justified by faith in Christ; of which faith the observance of these ceremonies was a sort of profession, inasmuch as they foreshadowed Christ."

68 Humbert, *Dialogus,* Will, 141.

69 Thus Nicholas Cabasilas, *De vita in Christo,* 1, PG 150, col 508.

70 Leo IX, *Ep. ad Michaelem Constantinopolitanum* I, Will, 68, 73-4.

71 Ibid. 70.

72 Ibid. 71.

73 Ibid. 77-8.

74 Ed *Humbert und Kerullarios* II, 416-75.

75 *De azymo et fermentato,* PL 158, cols 541-2.

76 Mansi, vol 23, col 295.

77 Ibid.
78 Synod in Trullo canon 11; Council of Laodicea canon 38.
79 Apostolic Canon 66: "If any of the clergy be found fasting on the Lord's Day, or on the Sabbath ... let him be deposed."
80 The Latin translation of Dionysius Exiguus included only the first fifty of the Apostolic Canons. The Synod in Trullo was originally rejected in Rome and only gradually did six of its 102 canons enter Western canonical collections.
81 The relevant canons are first pulled together in Stethatus' *Libellus*, Will, 133, and are set forward more elaborately by John II of Kiev, *Ep. ad Clementem* [anti-] *Papam*, ed Pavlov, 169-86.
82 Ibid.
83 *Responsio*, Will, 148.
84 *Dialogus*, Will, 119ff.
85 Dic. Grat. 4 post c. 13, D. 28.
86 Thus John II of Kiev, *op. cit.*
87 Stethatus, *Libellus*, Will, 130.
88 *De azymis contra Latinos*, ed Leib, "Deux inédits ...," 224-45. On Symeon's character, see Leib's introduction, 188-9.
89 Ibid. 245.
90 Leo of Ochrid, *Ep. ad Ioannem Tranensem*, Will, 56-7.
91 Euthymius Zigabenus, *Panoplia*, PG 130, col 1181.
92 Symeon of Jerusalem, *op. cit.* 226ff.
93 Jugie, *Theologia Dogmatica* III, 232-41.
94 Ibid.
95 *Ep. ad Domenicum Gradensem*, Will, 218.
96 *Panoplia*, PG 130, col 1180.
97 Ware, 114.
98 On the Leucius legend see Leib, "Deux inédits ...," 166.
99 Ware, 119.

Chapter 10

Filioque and the Fathers at the
Council of Florence*

No single event or issue divided the churches of East and West in the
Middle ages in the way that, e.g., Chalcedon and its christological
dogma divided the churches of antiquity. While the events of 1054 suggest
how far apart the churches had drifted, they hardly marked the consum-
mation of the schism, as historians like Gibbon once claimed. Almost at
once, new negotiations began. Even after growing animosity culminated
in the sack of Constantinople by the Fourth Crusade (1204), many
churchmen in the East—including conservative monastic circles—continued to view the schism as a temporary estrangement. Needed, in their
view, was free discussion of doctrinal issues at a true ecumenical council:
a common council duly convened in accordance with the practice of the
early Church at which all the churches, epitomized in the pentarchy of
patriarchates, would be represented.[1]

Appeals for such a council at first fell on deaf ears in the West, where
reunion was understood to be simply a matter of Byzantine submission
without reservation to the Roman see. But with the rise of conciliarism,
Greek initiatives met with a more favorable response. The result was the
Council of Ferrara/Florence (1438-9). In a sense, its convocation marks
the culmination of late medieval Greek efforts to achieve a reunion of the
churches. At the same time, its ultimate failure to achieve that objective
signals the end of the old Christian *oikoumenê*. The sense of mutual
interiority—of common participation in the mystery of the Church—

* A paper delivered at the conference on "Conciliarism and Conciliarity in the Late Middle Ages:
Perspectives East and West," at the Center for Medieval Studies, Fordham University, March
26, 1983.

which had persisted even after 1054 gives way to a sense of mutual exteriority, a sense that the other is "outside the Church."

In the Greeks' understanding, a true ecumenical council required not only representation of all churches—ecumenicity in space, as it were—but also ecumenicity in time: it had to be in continuity with and based upon the teachings of the ecumenical councils of antiquity and of the fathers. As early as 1419, the patriarch and the emperor were insisting that debate at a future ecumenical council should be based upon "the testimonies and citations of the holy teachers of the Church;"[2] and in 1434 Eugenius IV's ambassador to Constantinople, Christopher Garatoni, gave assurances that this would be the case.[3] What this meant for the Greeks can be seen at Ferrara when, in imitation of procedure at Ephesus and Chalcedon, they insisted on reading into the record a comprehensive dossier of authoritative conciliar decisions before any debate took place. It can also be seen at Florence in Mark Eugenicus' long speech during session six: abandoning the question-and-answer approach of earlier sessions, he produced a vast collection of quotations from scripture and the fathers held together with the barest minimum of commentary. What the fathers said was authoritative. At a true ecumenical council, therefore, recitation counted for more than argumentation.

The Latins, on the other hand, were more accustomed to scholastic debate. John Montenero in particular seems to have delighted in long disquisitions on *substantia prima* and *secunda* and other such metaphysical subtleties. For this approach the Greeks had little appreciation. According to the pro-unionist Isidore of Kiev, the Latins' syllogisms "have rather deepened the schism and have made the disagreement greater and stronger."[4] Syropoulos records the impression made on one of the Georgian envoys when Montenero appealed to the authority of Aristotle:

> He said: "Why Aristotle, Aristotle? Aristotle is no good." To the question which I posed to him by word and gesture, "What *is* good?" the Georgian replied: "St Peter, St Paul, St Basil, Gregory the Theologian, Chrysostom—not Aristotle, Aristotle!"[5]

Yet Montenero too could appeal to the authority of the fathers, and he could muster abundant citations from their works in support of his syllogistic argumentation—as in session seven, during which he presented eight hours of patristic testimony in support of his position.

Montenero's appeal to the fathers was decisive in convincing a number of the leading Greeks of the correctness of the Latin position. Bessarion later was to write:

> It was not the syllogisms or the cogency of proofs or the force of arguments that led me to believe this, but the plain words of the doctors. For when I saw and heard them, straightway I put aside all contention and controversy and yielded to the authority of those whose words they were, even though till then I had been not a little active in opposition. For I judged that the holy fathers, speaking as they did in the Holy Spirit, could not have departed from the truth...[6]

Bessarion, of course, may have been particularly open to persuasion. But at the time, most of his compatriots seem to have been equally convinced by Montenero's presentation. This is how George Scholarius, later a vigorous opponent of the Florentine union, sums up the situation:

> ... you all see that the Latins have contended brilliantly for their faith, so that no one with a sense of justice has any reason to reproach them... They brought forward from the common fathers of the Church the six most renowned in dignity, wisdom and struggles for the faith... as witnesses of their doctrine, each of whom must be judged the equal of all the men in the world, and those not just incidentally and casually but as if they were for us judges of the present disputes... Besides, they put forward others from the common fathers, those of the East I mean, adorned with an equal wisdom and honor, who also said just the same as those others, though not so plainly, if their words are examined in a spirit of truth and wisdom, and they offered in proof of their doctrine no merely specious reasoning, no coercion, but everything straightforwardly and as flowing from the divine scriptures and the fathers. On our part nothing was said to them to which they did not manifestly reply with wisdom, magnanimity and truth as we have no saint at all who clearly contradicts them. If indeed there were such, he should in some fashion or manner be made to harmonize with the majority... Nor shall we say that the doctors are mutually contradictory, for this is to introduce complete confusion and to deny the whole of the faith. Who is so simple-minded as to believe that the Latins wish to destroy the faith and to adulterate the trinitarian theology of all the doctors? Surely a man who affirms this deserves nothing but ridicule...[7]

Only Mark Eugenicus remained unmoved. With the others he believed that the fathers cannot contradict each other. But neither can they contradict the true faith. Therefore the texts advanced by the Latins must be corrupt, interpolated or in some other way falsified.

Bessarion, for one, found Mark's contention ridiculous: if all the words and phrases supporting the Latin position were removed from the books, we would be left with nothing but blank pages![8] Quite a few modern writers have agreed with Bessarion. Fr Joseph Gill, for example, in his many learned works on Florence always conveys the impression that Latin use of the fathers at Florence was appropriate, convincing and substantially accurate, so that any intelligent person of good will can but assent to the doctrines expressed in the council's decrees. For Fr Gill, therefore, the Council of Florence was a success that failed—failed above all because of the "intransigence" and "intractability" of Mark of Ephesus, "obdurate," "narrowminded" and "impervious to argument."[9] As he concludes, "If some one cause is to be assigned for the failure of the Council of Florence, that cause was Mark Eugenicus, metropolitan of Ephesus."[10] Some more recent presentations have taken a subtler approach. For example, a systematic study of the problem of ecclesiastical unification has described the Florentine union as an example of the "premature union," a union for which the "faithful masses" were "psychologically unprepared."[11] Yet the basic contention remains the same: Florence was a success that failed. At the risk of appearing "obdurate," "narrowminded" and as "deserving nothing but ridicule," I should like to argue the contrary: Florence was a failure that almost succeeded. And it was a failure precisely because of the way in which the fathers were presented, read and understood at the council itself.

To be sure, Mark's theory of wholesale fabrication is rather farfetched. Yet spurious texts did play a certain role in the "success" of the council, particularly in the way in which the crucial problem of the procession of the Holy Spirit was addressed. At Ferrara, the Greeks had sought to limit debate to the question of the *legality* of the Latin addition of the expression *filioque* ("and from the Son") to creed's words about the procession of the Holy Spirit ("And in the Holy Spirit, the Lord and giver of life, who proceeds from the Father"). Mark Eugenicus and Bessarion had forcefully argued that the Third Ecumenical Council (Ephesus 431) had categorically prohibited any addition to the creed, however true or worthy. The Latins therefore should drop the *filioque* regardless of the theological merits of their teaching on the procession. Of Cardinal Caesarini's counterarguments, particularly effective, at least with Bessarion, was the claim that the Council of Nicea itself had forbidden any change in the creed in terms virtually identical to those of Ephesus, yet as all acknowledged the next council, Constantinople, modified the original Nicene creed considerably. The documentation for the cardinal's claim: a letter of Pseudo-Liberius, drawn from the ninth-century Pseudo-Isidorian decretals.

Caesarini, of course, was not deliberately trying to deceive. Yet here, as on several other occasions, the Greeks were left looking foolish, whereas in fact the Latins were in error. Consider in this regard the long and acrimonious debate over the correct text of Basil the Great's treatise *Against Eunomius* III, 1-3.[12] The text upheld by the Latins read:

> Even if the Holy Spirit is third in dignity and order, why need he be third also in nature? For that he is second to the Son, *having his being from him and receiving from him and announcing to us and being completely dependent on him*, pious tradition recounts; but that his nature is third we are not taught by the saints nor can we conclude from what has been said...

The text upheld by the Greeks, on the other hand, included no such suggestion of dependence of the Holy Spirit on the Son:

> Even if the Holy Spirit is third in dignity and order, why need he be third also in nature? For that he is second to the Son pious tradition *perhaps* recounts; but that his nature is third we are not taught by the saints nor can we conclude from what has been said.

Interpolation or deletion? According to Mark, there were some thousand copies in Constantinople which agreed with his text and only a few—four or five—that followed the Latins'. Montenero, however, defended the veracity of his own book: it had been brought from Constantinople very recently by Nicholas of Cusa and therefore had not been in Latin hands long enough for it to have been tampered with, and besides, it was very old. Further, corruption of texts was more typical of the East than of the West; very likely the change was made in the early days of the schism in order to remove St Basil from the ranks of those favoring the traditional (i.e., the Latin) doctrine of the procession of the Holy Spirit. Then Montenero dramatically displayed both copies, his own written on parchment, Mark's obviously newer and written on paper. (A few days later he was able to strengthen his case further, by bringing in a very old codex belonging to the Greek Metropolitan Dorotheus of Mitylene which agreed with his text.)

Mark in reply admitted that Montenero's text was to be found in a few books in Constantinople, and the fact that these had not been destroyed proved the Greeks' honesty. The West, however, had done its share of fabrication. No less a person than Pope Zosimus had tried to impose on the Africans a supposed canon of Nicea that gave Rome universal rights as a court of appeal. The Africans, however, had compared their version of Nicea with those preserved in Alexandria and Constantinople and found that no such canon existed. Montenero in his turn questioned Mark's assertion concerning Zosimus. The Latins had never heard of such an episode, and Mark had not—and could not—produce a supporting document. The documents lay rather on the Latin side, as Cardinal Caesarini had shown in Ferrara when he exhibited that codex containing Pope Liberius' letter about Nicea.

What are we to make of this exchange? Here, as at many points, Mark's knowledge of church history in fact is far more accurate than the Latins'. His Zosimus story is substantially correct, though the pope in question appears to have been honestly mistaken: in the Roman archives the canons of Sardica, including the famous appeal canons, had been transcribed immediately after the canons of Nicea and numbered sequentially with them.[13] Scholars now are also inclined to accept Mark's version of the disputed passage from St Basil. The oldest Greek manuscripts of the text are divided, but a Syriac paraphrase, dating from a period well before the procession of the Holy Spirit became a disputed subject between East and West, agrees with Mark's version. According to the most recent treatment of the subject, *both* versions circulated in antiquity: the shorter version is authentically Basil's; the longer—expressing a teaching altogether uncharacteristic of that father—in fact interpolates a scholion extracted from a work by Eunomius, the very heretic against whom Basil's treatise was written![14]

Obviously we cannot blame Montenero and his associates for making honest mistakes due to the limitations of their historical scholarship. Indeed, an honest modern scholar must give them credit for that historical sense which led them to seek out the oldest manuscripts in the first place. This episode is significant not because one side was right and another wrong concerning a matter of fact but rather because it suggests how important—but also how potentially misleading—the appeal to patristic authority was at Florence. All agreed that we must look to the fathers, but in the absence of a common living tradition, this meant looking above all to the words of the fathers (preferably as preserved in the oldest manuscripts) rather than to their message. And their words were hard to come by. Today's scholar can "let his fingers do the walking" through the yellowed pages of Migne's patrology. At Ferrara-Florence, documentation was more difficult. After each public session, the speakers from both sides would meet with interpreters and notaries. A speaker who had quoted from councils or the fathers had to produce his codices for the inspection of the other side, and the notaries had to establish an accurate and mutually agreed upon record of what had been said. But trustworthy codices were few. A mutual lending arrangement was set up—one hour circulation! Florence and other cities of north-central Italy were ransacked for books. A friend of Ambrogio Traversari even extended the search to England.[15] In time, however, both sides came to rely more and more on *florilegia* to document their positions. Petit has edited a little collection of passages from scripture and the Greek fathers which Mark seems to have used during the council,[16] and Ortiz de Urbina has closely described a *florilegium*, probably assembled by Ambrogio Traversari, of quotations from the Greek fathers and the Latin fathers translated into Greek which almost certainly was the basis for much of Montenero's patristic argument at Florence.[17] Others certainly exist or at least once existed.[18]

In gathering such *florilegia* and other formal sources, the Latins had a distinct advantage. They could work as the council proceeded. The Greeks, on the other hand, had to have their homework substantially complete before leaving Constantinople. What formal sources could they have used? What formal sources did they use? Here it is possible to give only the barest survey of the Greeks' resources and potential resources as they relate to the most serious dogmatic issue facing the council: the procession of the Holy Spirit.

In the ninth century Photius, following the personalism of the Cappadocian fathers, had argued that the Spirit proceeds from the Father alone (*ek tou patros monou*). To maintain a double procession as the Franks did would confuse the personal (hypostatic) life of God with the divine essence, resulting in a kind of modalism. But what of patristic texts which speak of the Spirit as proceeding from the Father through the Son (*ek tou patros dia tou hyiou*)? Photius would take such expressions as referring to the temporal mission of the Spirit. In the thirteenth century, however, unionist Patriarch John Beccus, on the basis of an impressive dossier of patristic texts, had argued that more must be meant by the phrase; that in fact *ek* and *dia* were equivalent; thus that the Latins were correct in asserting the procession of Spirit from the Father and from the Son.

Alternative explanations, often mutually complementary, were advanced to explain the phrase. George Moschobar, for example, took the preposition *dia* as synonymous with *sun* or *meta* with the genitive complement: the Spirit proceeds from the Father with the Son, along with him quasi-simultaneously, just as word and breath issue forth from a man. A rather deeper explanation was put forward by Beccus' great adversary, Gregory of Cyprus, who distinguished between the hypostatic existence of the Holy Spirit, proceeding from the Father alone, and his eternal radiance or natural manifestation, which is from the Father through the Son. Unlike Photius, therefore, Gregory allowed for the possibility of eternal relations of Son and Spirit, even though, like Photius, he recognized that Son and Spirit are not, in their personal existence, determined by these relations.[19]

What Gregory of Cyprus allowed as a possibility, Gregory Palamas in the next century began to explore more deeply. Thus he can write:

> The Spirit of the Word from on high is like a mysterious love of the Father towards the Word mysteriously begotten: it is the same love as that possessed by the Word and well-beloved Son of the Father towards him who begat him; this he does insofar as he comes from the Father conjointly with this love and this love rests, naturally, on him.[20]

Palamas of course is not referring here to the Spirit's causal existence, to the procession *kath hyparksin* from the Father alone, but rather to the procession *kat' energeian*. But for Palamas that energy is not created but uncreated. That love which is manifested in time coming out from the Father through the Son in the Holy Spirit, which even we can experience, exists eternally in God.

The pneumatology of Gregory Palamas as anticipated by Gregory of Cyprus has been given favorable attention by modern theologians who see in it a possible way out of the futile old debates over the *filioque*.[21] It addresses the legitimate Western concern about the ultimate relation of Son and Spirit without "confusing the persons," i.e., without making the worship of God the Trinity into an impersonal monotheism. Of all the Eastern expositions of the procession of the Holy Spirit available at the time of Florence, it would seem to offer the greatest possibilities for theological advance. Unfortunately, the thought of the two Gregories was not expounded at Ferrara-Florence. If anything, it was deliberately avoided.

In preparation for Florence, the Greeks carefully studied particularly Nilus Cabasilas' treatise on the procession of the Holy Spirit, and at least at the beginning of the council it was most often the "formal source" of their arguments and patristic proof-texts.[22] After the debates over the legality of the addition proved inconclusive, Bessarion confidently urged debate on the doctrine of the procession itself:

> We can say a great deal and say it well about the faith, and we ought not cower before the Latins. Cabasilas wrote only four pages on the addition, yet what we have said about it here would fill a book. On the doctrine he wrote a whole book, and so surely we shall be able to say a very great deal.[23]

What are the characteristics of Nilus Cabasilas' treatise? The author had once been an ardent admirer of Thomas Aquinas, whose works he knew through the translations of Demetrius Cydones, but later he was a firm opponent. The treatise was a point-by-point response to Aquinas' arguments for the Latin doctrine of the procession. Cabasilas is frequently believed to have been very sympathetic to Palamism. Indeed, many of his arguments can be found in Palamas' works, but for the most part these are the common stock of anti-unionist theologians since the time of Beccus. The distinctive elements of Palamas' pneumatology do not emerge in his treatise. For example, the love analogy mentioned earlier is explicitly rejected.[24] In fact, Nilus Cabasilas' overall approach as well as specific arguments owe much more to Palamas' opponent, Barlaam the Calabrian: we cannot know God as he really is; therefore all the Latins' fine reasoning is simply a sign of presumption.[25] By basing themselves on Nilus Cabasilas, the Greeks thus were well equipped for negative arguments but not for a positive presentation of the procession or for any theological advance or breakthrough.

It is hardly surprising that Bessarion, already swayed by Caesarini's Pseudo-Liberius and by Montenero's appeal to the fathers, turned from Cabasilas' treatise to Beccus' *Epigraphae* and, from April 1439, argued the equivalence of the prepositions *ek* and *dia*, thus with the Latins recognizing the Son as mediate cause of the Spirit. But what of Mark Eugenicus? He is usually regarded as in the Palamite tradition, and in his *Capita syllogistica,* written after his return to Constantinople, he shows a very good acquaintance with Palamas' basic ideas on pneumatology, albeit expressing these in a largely negative way. For example, he regularly and clearly distinguished the procession *kat' energeian* from the procession *kath hyparksin* and castigates the partisans of *filioque* for their failure to do so.[26] But this pneumatology by no means comes through in the acts or other sources of the Council of Florence. An explanation for this may lie in the fact that the Greek delegation at Florence was itself divided over the subject of Palamism generally. For example, Bessarion had been expressing doubts about Palamas' distinction between essence and energies well before he espoused the Latin doctrine on the procession of the Holy Spirit.[27] Or perhaps the Greeks realized that the Latins, and particularly Dominicans like Montenero, would have little sympathy for Palamas' theology. At any rate, in the sixth session at Florence, when Montenero began asking Mark about his understanding of the relationship between the Holy Spirit and his gifts, the emperor ordered Mark to drop the subject, to forestall (as the Greek Acts note) "disputation on the question of created or uncreated [energies]."[28]

Florence, I asserted earlier, is less a success that failed than a failure that almost succeeded. At the council, both sides relied on assembling proof-texts, claiming for these isolated words the full message and authority of the fathers. This hardly is the mark of success. And in the process both sides failed to advance discussion of the substantive dogmatic issues which divided the churches. The Latins were oblivious to the basic intuitions and concerns of the Greek patristic tradition and even to many aspect of the Latin tradition. Misjudging the weight and consistency of their some-times questionable sources, they sought only to fit the theology of others into their own narrow system. The Greeks, on the other hand, internally divided and perhaps afraid of real theological discussion, retreated to the defensive position established by an earlier generation of controversialists. Overconfidence and failure of confidence, both appealing to the fathers: such ironies abound at Florence. But perhaps one more should be men-tioned. In the course of conciliar proceedings, only one Greek theologian from after the schism of the churches was cited by name. After all, authority lay with the common fathers of antiquity. That theologian:

Gregory Palamas. The speaker: from the Latin side. The message: "We must not behave in unseemly fashion, vainly quarreling about words."[29]

NOTES

1 On this subject see especially D. M. Nicol, "Byzantine Requests for an Oecumenical Council in the Fourteenth Century," *Annuarium historiae conciliorum* 1 (1969) 69-95, now conveniently included in his collected essays, *Byzantium: Its Ecclesiastical History and Relations with the Western World* (Variorum, London 1972); J. Meyendorff, "What is an Ecumenical Council?" *St. Vladimir's Theological Quarterly* 17 (1973) 259-73, now included in his *Living Tradition: Orthodox Witness in the Contemporary World* (St. Vladimir's Seminary Press, Crestwood, NY 1978) 45-62; A. Papadakis, "Ecumenism in the Thirteenth Century: The Byzantine Case," *St. Vladimir's Theological Quarterly* 27 (1983) 207-17; J. Boojamra, "The Transformation of Conciliar Theory in the Last Century of Byzantium," *St. Vladimir's Theological Quarterly* 31 (1987) 215-35; and, from the earlier literature, G. Hofmann, "L'idea del concilio ecumenico come mezzo d'unione nelle trattative fra Bisanzio e Roma," *Unitas* 5 (1950) 17-28.

2 See Syropoulos, *Memoirs* 2.8, ed V. Laurent, *Les "Memoires" du Grand Ecclesiarque de l'Eglise de Constantinople Sylvestre Syropoulos sur le concile de Florence (1438-1439)* (Centre National de la Recherche Scientifique, Paris 1971) 110.4-6.

3 *Epistolae pontificiae ad Concilium Florentinum spectantes* I, ed G. Hofmann (Rome 1940) 40.3-4.

4 Quoted from codex Vat. Gr. 706, ff 12r-22r, by J. Gill, *The Council of Florence* (Cambridge 1961) 227.

5 *Memoirs* 9.28, ed Laurent, 464.16-8.

6 *De Spiritus Sancti processione ad Alexium Lascarin Philanthropinum*, ed E. Candal (Rome 1961) 40.11-41.5; cf. the hermeneutical principle—in fact shared by all the Greeks at Florence—which Bessarion, quoting St John of Damascus, sets forth in his *Oratio dogmatica de Unione* 2.5 (12), ed E. Candal (Rome 1958) 13.1-9: "The saints must mutually agree. They cannot oppose and contradict each other, for the power and illumination of the same one Spirit have brought it about that their opinion in matters pertaining to the faith is one and the same." See also J. Madoz, "El Argumento Patristico segun Bessarion in Florencia," *Gregorianum* 15 (1934) 215-41.

7 In his speech to the Greeks at Florence "On the Need of Aiding Constantinople," ed L. Petit *et al.*, *Oeuvres complètes de Gennade Scholarios*, vol 1 (Paris 1928) 297-9, trans Gill, *Council*, 225-6.

8 *Quae supersunt actorum graecorum Concilii Florentini*—cited hereafter as *Acta Graeca*—ed J. Gill (Rome 1953) 401.20-2.

9   Quoted here: *Personalities of the Council of Florence* (Blackwell, Oxford 1964)
    256, 262, 63, 64, 61.

10 Ibid. 64. For a very different evaluation of Mark of Ephesus see C. Tsirpanlis,
    *Mark Eugenicus and the Council of Florence: A Historical Re-evaluation of His
    Personality* (Thessalonica 1974).

11 Thus J. Macha, *Ecclesiastical Unification: A Theoretical Framework Together
    With Case Studies From the History of Latin-Byzantine Relations* (=Orientalia
    Christiana Analecta 198, Rome 1974) especially 123-8, 141-3.

12 The exchange is recounted in Gill, *Council*, 199-205 *et passim*, with translation
    of the passage in question at 199n.

13 See H. Hess, *The Canons of the Council of Sardica, AD 343* (Oxford 1958)
    49-55, 151-2.

14 M. Van Parys, "Quelques remarques à propos d'un texte controversé de Saint
    Basile au Concile de Florence," *Irenikon* 40 (1967) 6-14.

15 On the problem of locating books for use at the council see Gill, *Council*, 163-5.

16 In *Patrologia Orientalis* 17, 342-67.

17 I. Ortiz de Urbina, "Un codice fiorentino di raccolte patristiche," *Orientalia
    Christiana Periodica* 4 (1938) 423-40, analyzing MS Conv. soppr. 603, Bibl.
    Med. -Laur.

18 See my "Greek Excerpts from the *Decretum*," *Bulletin of Medieval Canon Law* 1
    (1971) 86-7, which examines John Plousiadenus' *Expositio pro concilio
    Florentino*, PG 159, cols 1109-1394. Note also Escorial MS 36 (R.III.2.) as
    described in the *Catálogo de los códices griegos de la biblioteca de El Escorial* I
    (Madrid 1936) 145-8.

19 On the pneumatology of Gregory of Cyprus see especially the excellent study of
    A. Papadakis, *Crisis in Byzantium: The Filioque Controversy in the Patriarchate of
    Gregory II of Cyprus (1283-1289)* (Fordham, New York 1982), and the earlier
    work of O. Clement, "Gregoire du Chypre: De l'ekporèse du Saint Esprit,"
    Istina 27 (1972) 443-56. A convenient survey of the procession of the Holy
    Spirit in ancient and Byzantine Greek theology is provided by M. A. Orphanos,
    "The Procession of the Holy Spirit According to Certain Greek Fathers,"
    Theologia 50 (1979) 763-78; 51 (1980) 87-107, 276-99, 436-61; and more
    briefly by J. Meyendorff, "La Procession du Saint Esprit chez les Pères Ori-
    entaux," *Russie et Chrétienté* 2 (Istina, Boulogne-sur-Seine 1950) 158-78.

20 *Capita physica* 37, PG 150, cols 1144-5. On the pneumatology of Palamas see J.
    Meyendorff, *A Study of Gregory Palamas* (Faith Press, London 1964) 228-32
    and Orphanos, "The Procession," 436-46.

21 See, for example, the "Klingenthal Memorandum" of 1979, published in *Spirit
    of God, Spirit of Christ: Ecumenical Reflections on the Filioque Controversy*, ed L.
    Vischer (=Faith and Order Paper 103, WCC, Geneva 1981) 3-18.

22 E. Candal, "Opus ineditum Nili Cabasilae de Spiritus Sancti processione contra Latinos," *Orientalia Christiana Periodica* 9 (1943) 245-306.

23 Syropoulos, *Memoirs,* 7.12, ed Laurent, 362.11-14.

24 *De Spiritus Sancti processione* cap. 40, syl. 6, ed E. Candal, *Nilus Cabasilas et Theologia S. Thomae de Processione Spiritus Sancti* (=Studi e testi 116, Vatican City 1945) 310-25; cf. the editor's introduction.

25 Cf. *De Spiritus Sancti processione* prooemium, ed Candal, 208-12. On Nilus Cabasilas' relationship to Barlaam see also G. Schirò, "Il paradosso di Nilo Cabasila," *Studi bizantini* 9 (1957) 362-88.

26 *Capita syllogistica* 4, ed Petit, *Patrologia Orientalis* 15, 373. On the pneumatology of Mark see most conveniently Orphanos, "The Procession," 446-61.

27 See Gill, *Council,* 225. On the subject of Bessarion's religious convictions see also Fr Gill's articles on "The Sincerity of Bessarion the Unionist," *Journal of Theological Studies* 26 (1975) 377-92, and "Was Bessarion a Conciliarist or a Unionist before the Council of Florence?" *Collectanea Byzantina* (=Orientalia Christiana Analecta 204, Rome 1977) 201-19.

28 *Acta Graeca,* 346.8-12.

29 Andrew Chrysoberges (the Dominican Latin bishop of Rhodes), *Acta Graeca,* 102.27-103.9.

Index